Masonry in Architecture

Louis G. Redstone, FAIA

McGRAW-HILL BOOK COMPANY
New York St. Louis San Francisco Auckland Bogotá
Hamburg Johannesburg London Madrid Mexico
Montreal New Delhi Panama Paris São Paulo
Singapore Sydney Tokyo Toronto

To my sons, Daniel and Eliel, and my grandson, Adam

Library of Congress Cataloging in Publication Data

Redstone, Louis G.
  Masonry in architecture.

  Includes index.
  1. Masonry. 2. Architecture, Modern—20th century.
  3. Decoration and ornament, Architectural. I. Title.
NA4119.R42   1984   721'.0441   83-7946
ISBN 0-07-051387-2

1234567890   HAL/HAL   89876543

ISBN 0-07-051387-2

*The editors for this book were Joan Zseleczky and Christine Ulwick,
the designer was Naomi Auerbach, and the production
supervisor was Reiko F. Okamura. It was set in Melior
by Progressive Typographers.*

Printed and bound by Halliday Lithograph.

Contents

FOUR   Masonry as an Art Form   115

FIVE   Technical Aspects of Masonry Design   155

Preface

The main purpose of this book is to focus attention on the innovative uses of brick, an age-old material, and of concrete units, a material of this century. What makes brick the building material used consistently since the beginning of civilization? The availability of clay deposits and the tropical sun lead to the natural development of making small brick units for shelters. Thus the smallest building module was created over 5000 years ago and has had a history of continuous use to this day. The methods of production however have changed dramatically. A brief history of how brick was made and used from the early cultures to the present day is given in the first chapter.

It is my intention to illustrate in this book how buildings constructed of these modules not only answer the present-day needs of function and aesthetics, but also evoke a feeling of closeness and warmth. Brick and masonry units are of a size that enables many people to relate comfortably with the human scale. What makes its use so desirable is its adaptability to design forms, richness in texture, its modern adaptation for structural requirements of high-rise buildings, minimum maintenance, and cost competitiveness with other materials. Masonry also plays a significant role in the rapidly expanding movement of restoring and preserving old buildings of historical and design value.

This book presents a wide variety of significant current buildings encompassing all types of functions: residential, commercial, educational, health care, industrial, and recreational. Many of the examples are award winners and are accompanied by descriptive material. Separate chapters are devoted to projects in the United States and Canada, and in a number of countries around the world.

A chapter on the use of masonry as an art form features examples of masonry units integrated with the building elements—bas-relief murals of standard size units, premolded or carved brick murals, and freestanding sculpture works. Included also is the use of brick in shaping landscape and environmental forms. The last chapter deals with important technical elements necessary in the decision making for successful design implementation.

The examples presented were chosen to show the wide range of the inherent design possibilities for the architects, engineers, designers, developers, artists, masons, city planners and government officials, as well as the general public.

It is my hope that this book will be helpful in achieving this goal.

Louis G. Redstone

Acknowledgments

In preparing this book, I am deeply indebted to the many members of the architectural profession and the architectural societies, as well as the masonry institutes in the United States, Canada, and Europe.

My appreciation goes to the contributors to Chapter 5 on technical aspects. They are Ralph J. Stephenson, P.E., consultant engineer; William Lefkowski, P.E., structural engineer; Leo G. Shea, FAIA, president of Louis G. Redstone Associates, Architects & Engineers; and Donald J. Smith, CSI, architect and associate of the Redstone firm.

I am thankful to John A. Heslip, executive director, and Ronald S. Hurta of the Michigan Masonry Institute for their encouragement and assistance; to Morgan K. Fields of Tennessee and Norbert J. Hyneck of Wisconsin and to Colin Munro of Illinois, director of their state institutes.

Also of assistance were the Brick Institute of America and their regional offices; Ray Lackey, executive director, and Melissa Maholick of the International Masonry Institute; Richard W. Daly, director of communications and education of the International Union of Bricklayers and Allied Craftsmen; Royal Architectural Institute of Canada; Mrs. Marie-Anne Evans, assistant to the director of the Museum of Modern Art; Martin Filler, editor of *House & Garden Magazine*; Deborah Allen, acting assistant convenor, Jack Kennedy, Linda Safran, editor of the Aga Khan Award for Architecture; Fred Bassetti, of Bassetti, Norton, Metler, Architects P.S., Seattle, Washington; Mara Smith, sculptress in brick of Waterville, Illinois; Professors Bernard and Norma Goldman of Wayne State University, Detroit, Michigan, for historical background and photos; Basil Saffer, director of General Shale Products Corporation, Johnson City, Tennessee; Balthazar Korab, photographer, Troy, Michigan; Mary Randlett, photographer, Bainbridge Island, Washington.

Valuable resource material from a number of European countries came from professional masonry organizations, architectural societies, and editors of professional magazines as well as individual architects and sculptors. These include J. J. Beljon, director, Royal Academy of Fine Arts at The Hague, Holland; Dr. Justus Dahinden, honorary FAIA, Zurich, Switzerland; Vaquero Turcios, sculptor, Madrid, Spain; Pierre Szekely, sculptor, Paris, France; G. Peirs, director of Groupement National De L'Industrie, De La Terre Cuite, Belgium; E. R. L. Edwards, the Brick Development Association, Windsor, Berkshire, England; R. H. Kamen, the British Architectural Library, Royal Institute of British Architects, London, England; John H. Gailer, honorary editor, Society of Architectural and Associated Technicians, London, England; Ulla Sintonen, editorial secretary for *Tiili*, technical magazine on architecture, Helsinki, Finland; Maurice Merian, director of Federation Des Fabricants De Tuiles, et De Briques De France, Paris, France; W. N. van Batenburg, *Baksteen* Magazine, Ubbergen, Holland; Esben Madsen, Mun Sentret, Oslo, Norway; Charles McKean, the Royal Incorporation of Architects in Scotland; Keller Ag Ziegelein, Zurich, Switzerland.

Special thanks go to my secretarial assistant Gloria Barnabo Tonelli and to my wife Ruth whose assistance in research and editing made the preparation of this book a pleasant and stimulating experience.

CHAPTER ONE

Masonry in Various Civilizations

According to archaeologists, the use of brick as a building material goes back over 5000 years. It developed in areas where there was a scarcity of wood and stone, but an abundance of clay deposits. It was here that people first learned to use the clay to make bricks, and some of the oldest and most beautiful examples of brick architecture are found in the regions of the Tigris-Euphrates valleys and the Nile Valley.

Alluvial clay in the Nile Valley was used by the early Egyptians to make the sun-dried brick from which they built their dwellings. By 4000 B.C. they had acquired the use of copper for making tools. This allowed the Egyptians to perfect materials and construction methods which were quite sophisticated for their time (Figure 1). The pyramid near the city of Memphis, the first capital of Egypt, was the forerunner of the later large Cheops pyramid. Built of sandstone and brick, this pyramid is constructed in terraced steps (Figure 2).

Although stone was widely used in early Egyptian buildings, brick was one of the primary materials for all types of structures. The use of masonry has continued through the centuries to modern times. In Egypt, even now, some of the old processes of making brick are still being used. First the bricks are left to dry in the sun. Then they are taken through the kiln. One can see this on the road from Memphis to Cairo, where there are a large number of brick manufacturing plants (see Figures 3 and 4). Masonry skills can also be seen in the old quarters of Cairo. There the walls, the street and courtyard paving, and the steps leading to the buildings are made of masonry units (Figures 5 and 6). Here are located the historic Jewish synagogue and the early Coptic church.

The civilizations of Sumeria and Akkad (ca. 4000 to 1275 B.C.), Assyria (1275 to 612 B.C.), and Persia (538 to 330 B.C.) developed on the plains of Mesopotamia and Iran and produced great cities such as Babylon, Ur of the Chaldees, and Persepolis. The famous Ziggurat of Dur Kurigalzu in western

Figure 1. Egyptian masons at work, from a fresco of an ancient tomb. (Photo: Courtesy of Basil Saffer, curator, General Shale Museum of Ancient Brick)

Figure 2. Pyramid at Memphis, Egypt. The forerunner of the later Cheops pyramids. (Photographer: Louis G. Redstone)

Figure 3. Present-day brick manufacturing in Egypt. Sun drying of bricks prior to going through the kiln. (Photographer: Louis G. Redstone)

Figure 4. (Top) Present-day kiln, located on the road from Memphis to Cairo. (Photographer: Louis G. Redstone)

Figure 5. (Bottom left) Brick work detail in the old Cairo quarters. (Photographer: Louis G. Redstone)

Figure 6. (Bottom right) Close-up brick detail work in the old Cairo quarters. (Photographer: Louis G. Redstone)

Figure 7. "Apartment house," Mohejo-Daro, Pakistan, 2000 B.C., located in the Indus Valley of modern Pakistan. (Photographer: Bernard Goldman)

Figure 8. Processional wall of one Ishtar gate. Palace of Nebuchadnezzer in Babylon (now Iraq). (Photographer: Richard Ahern)

Iran (1400 B.C.) was built of sun-dried bricks and faced with baked bricks, the remains of which still stand. Sun-dried bricks were also used in Pakistan as seen in the remains of "apartment buildings" at Mohenjo-Daro, dating to the second millennium B.C. (Figure 7). In Babylon (604 B.C.) in the palace of Nebuchadnezzar in the processional wall of the Ishtar gate, brick bas-reliefs formed an integral part (Figure 8). Multicolor glazed brick reliefs depicting lions were also used in his throne room. The excellent design and skillfulness serve as an inspiration for using brick as a contemporary art material.

Another outstanding example is the palace complex of Persepolis, begun in the late sixth century B.C. It was constructed atop a 40-foot-high, manufactured earth platform, 1000 feet by 1500 feet, which was contained by an 11-foot stone retaining wall. On top of the platform, the 100-column hall of Xerxes was erected (Figure 9). The stone-carved columns and the retaining wall reliefs depict processions of the royal guard, tributary nations coming to the court, and the king enthroned. These are still admired today for their beauty, skill, and ingenuity. The walls of the Darius palace were built of sun-dried brick except for door frames, windows, and wall recesses, which were carved in stone and still remain intact today. In other Persian cities such as Shiraz and Isfahan, which were founded over a thousand years after Persepolis was built, were many examples of brick architecture showing the use of sun-dried and fire brick as well as stone work.

The growth and development of Greek civilization reached its "golden

Figure 9. Bas-relief carvings in the retaining walls of Xerxes temple at Persepolis (now Iran). (Photographer: Louis G. Redstone)

Figure 10. Acropolis, Athens, Greece, stone and brick masonry, faced with stone. (Photographer: Louis G. Redstone)

age" in the middle of the fifth century B.C. with the conquest of Alexander the Great. The temple of Zeus, the palace, the theater, the treasury, and other buildings made up the complex at Olympia, built between 700 and 300 B.C. The buildings on the Acropolis at Athens include the Parthenon, which was built of stone masonry, a material readily available (Figure 10). However, many of the structures were brick faced with stone, and in the earlier period many of the buildings were exposed brick.

As the political domination of the Mediterranean world shifted from Greece to Rome, the Romans assumed leadership in architecture as well as politics. They took Greek architecture, formalized it, and added engineering technology which produced the splendor of classical Rome.

Romans developed concrete, which made possible larger and more complicated structures than had been built by the Greeks. They used brick and concrete for structural walls, much like the grouted brick walls of today. An example of the capability of the Roman builders is the Coliseum, built in A.D. 70 (Figure 11). Even by today's standards this is an outstanding structure. It was an ellipse 620 feet by 513 feet overall with an arena 287 feet by 180 feet, with exterior walls 157½ feet high. The seating capacity was 80,000. There were three levels below the stands which contained hundreds of rooms for various purposes. The basic structure was brick faced with stone. In Rome many of the minor streets were lined with brick buildings. These were usually limited to minor structures because of a 75-foot height limitation established for all buildings except government buildings. In the area of the Bay of Naples, ruins of the city of Cumae, A.D. 200, show the extensive use of brick arches (Figure 12).

Figure 11. The Coliseum, Rome, A.D. 70, one of the most complex brick structures. (Photographer: Norma Goldman)

Figure 12. Ruins of the city of Cumae, near Naples (A.D. 200). Extensive use of brick arches. (Photographer: Bernard Goldman)

As the Roman culture moved to the east and merged with the Byzantine in Constantinople, bricks and glazed tile mosaics were materials used both structurally and decoratively in the arch and dome forms. An example of this is the famous Cathedral of Hagia Sophia. Its interior is an oval 250 feet by 220 feet, and the dome, which is 107 feet in diameter and a total of 180 feet high, is built of 27-inch-square brick, 2 inches thick.

The period between the fall of the Holy Roman Empire about A.D. 475 to the end of the twelfth century was enriched with the Romanesque style. The artisan's skills in brickwork advanced greatly. The Church of St. Vitale at Ravenna, Italy, built in A.D. 600, is an example of Italian Romanesque Figure 13). St. Antonia in Italy, built in the late thirteenth century, combines Romanesque, Byzantine, and Gothic details, and St. Paolo in Venice typifies the beauty of well-executed brick details. In the same period, other cultures utilized brick for temples, tomb towers, and fortress cities such as the Red City, Afghanistan, A.D. 1200 (Figure 14). Some of the most interesting structures still in use from the seventh century A.D. are in north Yemen in the cities of Umram and Viblah. Here, too, some are built of adobe brick, and the

Figure 13. (Below) Church of St. Vitale, Ravenna, Italy, A.D. 600. Example of Italian Romanesque. (Photographer: Bernard Goldman)

Figure 14. (Opposite) Red City, Afghanistan (A.D. 1200). (Photographer: Bernard Goldman)

Figure 15. Umram, north Yemen, farm complex (from seventh century). (Photographer: Balthazar Korab)

more elaborate are built of a combination of stone and brick (Figures 15 and 16).

The dawn of the fifteenth century was also the dawn of the Renaissance or rebirth of classical architecture. The construction methods and use of material developed during the Romanesque and Gothic periods were employed and adapted to the classical form. The grandeur of ancient Rome was recaptured in the Renaissance city planning as well as in its buildings. The Piazza of St. Peters in Rome is 650 feet wide. The cathedral is 600 feet by 450 feet and contains 227,070 square feet. Its masonry dome, supported on four great piers, starts 250 feet above the floor, is $137\frac{1}{2}$ feet in diameter, and 450 feet to the top.

As this style moved north and west from Italy, it picked up the warmth and beauty of red brick, particularly in Holland and England. Houses in Amsterdam show the combination of red brick and stone which was popular in northern Europe, England, and later in the new world.

The year of 1612 marks the beginning of brick-making in the first colonies in Jamestown, Virginia; 1628 in New Amsterdam. In 1629 the first kiln was erected in Salem, Massachusetts. Brick-makers from Holland and England were listed among the first immigrants and brought their methods to the new world. Wherever clay was available, the brickyard became part of the community's building resource. Wood for the firing of the brick was plentiful everywhere. It was only natural that brick was the favorite material for homes and community buildings in the colonies.

The settlers brought with them the background of English and European Renaissance architecture, and as soon as they moved beyond the log cabin stage they built permanent buildings. At Williamsburg, Virginia, the governor's palace and the capitol were examples of transplanted English Renaissance architecture. The bricks used were handmade. Monticello, the home of Thomas Jefferson, is a well-known example of colonial brick architecture.

Brick-making during the 5000 or more years of its history up to this point had changed very little. Mule power had been introduced, but the brick was still molded in wood molds and air dried. Crude wood- or coal-burning kilns

Figure 16. Viblah, north Yemen, A.D. 1100 to A.D. 1200. Stone buildings except minaret, which is of brick. (Photographer: Balthazar Korab)

had been developed, but the quality and character of the units had changed very little. The industrial revolution and its trend toward machines replacing human labor did not materially change the brick industry until the twentieth century. The periodic or "beehive" kiln and steam or electric power were the only significant changes until after World War II.

Mechanization and automation have been growing in the brick plant during the past twenty-five years. Machinery is used to mine and handle the clay, grind and blend the clays, and extrude and cut the clay into dense, precise units. The bricks are fired in continuous tunnel kilns at carefully controlled temperatures to produce the best unit that can be made from the clay used. The brick is inspected, sorted, and packaged for easy and safe shipment to the job site. Brick made in the United States is of high quality. It is precise, durable, strong, color-fast, and comes in literally thousands of combinations of sizes, shapes, colors, and textures.

The use of brick as a structural, load-bearing material also continued unchanged from its beginning through the nineteenth century. The development of structural steel and later reinforced concrete frame construction replaced the heavy brick bearing walls as load-carrying elements. During the first two-thirds of this century brick was used extensively as enclosure and exterior surface material, in combination with steel or concrete frame. With the development of engineering technology based on an extensive international testing program, tight quality control was developed. This know-how enabled the building of major structures with brick bearing walls.

The 1960s and 1970s showed the advancement in prefabrication methods. One method is to prefabricate in the plant and bring to the job site. These panels are fabricated in vertical position, using plain mortar with reinforcing steel for lifting only. Another method—prefabrication at the job site—can be done by using high-strength mortar additives. The panels then can be anchored to the concrete or steel frame of the building structure. Other job-site prefabrication methods are discussed in detail in the chapter on technical aspects.

Fine modern brickwork dates from the seventeenth century. Different bonding patterns were worked out, English and Flemish; later on, rowlock and soldier courses were introduced to create interest and accents in brick walls.

Handmade bricks, which contributed to the richness of texture and color, gave way because of economic factors to the standardized modular brick. Offsetting the qualities of handmade bricks were the developments of new tools such as diamond saws which could cut and shape the bricks on the job site.

During the period of 1930 to the middle 1950s, steel and concrete were the dominant materials for designers of structures. Since then, masonry, whether in the form of concrete units or bricks, is regaining its importance on the architects' boards. Structural characteristics, flexibility in design, ease of maintenance, and qualities such as fireproofing and waterproofing and above all its competitiveness with other materials raised the desirability for its use.

The flexibility in design of masonry materials is evident in the wide and varied range of excellent structures created in the 1970s. It is interesting to note that the architects involved in these projects represent a cross section of outstanding professionals from all parts of the United States. Similarly, the same recognition of the quality values of masonry is being experienced in Canada and the European countries. Also in the Islamic world, an impetus created by the yearly Aga Khan architecture-for-excellence competition is producing a renewed interest in masonry usage. The encouragement of skill in masonry was exemplified in the first prize award in 1980 being given to an elderly Egyptian master mason.

An important emerging element which adds a human touch and spark is the integration of masonry art forms as part of the structure as well as of the contiguous surroundings (plazas, walkways, play areas). Some architects consider their building designs as art forms in themselves and disregard the art element issue entirely; others work successfully with a number of artists in the initial stages of their designs. There is a growing expertise being developed by sculptors, here and abroad, to create bas-reliefs in exciting premolded and prefired brick murals. The colorful glazed brick mural as an integral part of the total design is also coming into its own.

Although the author considers masonry "a material for all time," the architect and engineer must carefully consider whether masonry units best relate to the geographic location and the surrounding structures, and can implement to advantage the design concept.

As great as are the advances that have been made to date in the masonry field, there is no doubt that we can expect further major technical and innovative developments.

CHAPTER TWO

The United States and Canada

This chapter presents a number of projects highlighting the various uses of masonry construction (brick and block). The examples shown are from various parts of the United States and Canada. Masonry is shown as a most adaptable material for new design forms. The ranges of shape, size, texture, color, and finishes are extensive. With the new technical advances in "engineered masonry," this material takes its place alongside other contemporary construction systems—steel, aluminum, glass, concrete. In addition, it dovetails well with all of these materials. The examples in this chapter illustrate the versatility of masonry.

KELMER ARLINGTON BUILDING
Arlington Heights, Illinois / 1973
ARCHITECT: Stanley Tigerman & Associates

ARCHITECT'S COMMENTS: The site was next to a rather more conventional industrial building. The small industrial park that was to house the building is located in direct proximity to the rather typical suburban single-family, freestanding, detached house. Whatever one may think of "Suburbia, USA," rather than subject its residents to so obvious a disparate use as industrial, it seemed somehow appropriate to make the building as abstract and nonbuildinglike as possible, that is, at once a sculpture as well as closely approximating the original intention in the first place. To accomplish this end it seemed fitting to develop a kind of scalelessness rather than to change the scale from the "front" (human scale) to the "back" (vehicular scale) and to, as best as practicable, detail the building as flush as possible, as if the skin were a decal.

With philosophic convolutions in hand, restrictive budgets resulted in the 22,000-square-foot masonry perimeter bearing wall. That solar bronze glass with directly glazed duranodic copings, radial brick, and other excesses not normally found in this building prototype were allowed to occur is the product of a great effort to reduce the basic spanning structure to an effective minimum —$47\frac{1}{2}$-foot-long span open-web steel joists supporting a metal deck above on a minimum of point supports based on girders welded at points of contraflexure, perimeter as bearing wall itself, no operating sash, rooftop comfort conditioning units, minimum steel linteling over masonry openings, and other devices contributed to that level of freedom which resulted in those above-mentioned factors that deal with approaching the original concept as a visual fact. The lack of any particular landscaping is not accidentally in support of the "abstract" concept; one more "scale device" is even removed by placing a narrow band of gravel at the edge of the building to confound grass from growing at the building's edge.

(Top) Close-up of exterior. (Photographer: Philip Turner)

(Bottom) Forming detail. (Photograph: Courtesy of Stanley Tigerman & Associates)

Exterior view. (Photographer: Philip Turner)

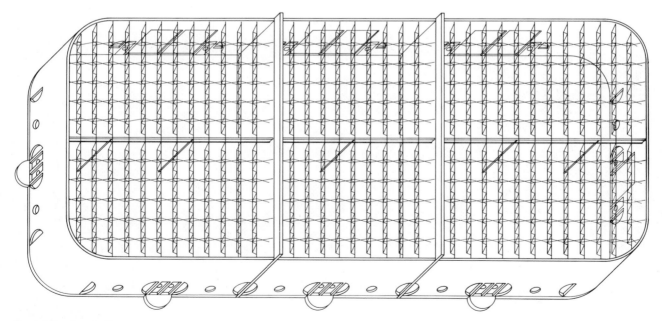

Isometric, plan section.

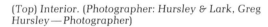

McDONALD'S RESTAURANT
Ann Arbor, Michigan / 1976
ARCHITECT: Hobbs & Black Associates, Inc.

ARCHITECT'S COMMENTS: The building is located within one block of the central campus of the University of Michigan. Its site was formerly occupied by an historically valued residence and is surrounded by several masonry buildings which are highly regarded by the community for their architectural and historical significance. The owner's commitment to respond to the area's historical needs is evidenced by the use of brick for interior and exterior walls, courtyard walls, and as a paving element. The sensitive detailing of the building forms and extensive soldier coursing lend to and enhance the scale and flavor of the historical architecture that is present in this pedestrian-commercial district.

(Top) Interior. (Photographer: Hursley & Lark, Greg Hursley—Photographer)

(Bottom) Exterior. (Photographer: Hursley & Lark, Greg Hursley—Photographer)

NORTHVILLE SQUARE CENTER
Northville, Michigan / 1973

ARCHITECT: Louis G. Redstone
Associates, Inc.

ARCHITECT'S COMMENTS: Northville Square was
originally planned as a shopping center and is
located in the heart of Northville, Michigan.
It is now converted into a wholesale gift mart.

The building has several unique
characteristics, including its location in the
center of an established urban area, not on the
periphery of an outlying suburban area.

The bilevel structure is of warm-toned brick
masonry, and its hillside location allows
entry from sidewalks at both shopping levels.

Exterior view. (Photographer: Balthazar Korab)

(*Right*) *Exterior view showing variation of levels.* (*Photographer: Balthazar Korab*)

(*Bottom*) *First floor plan.*

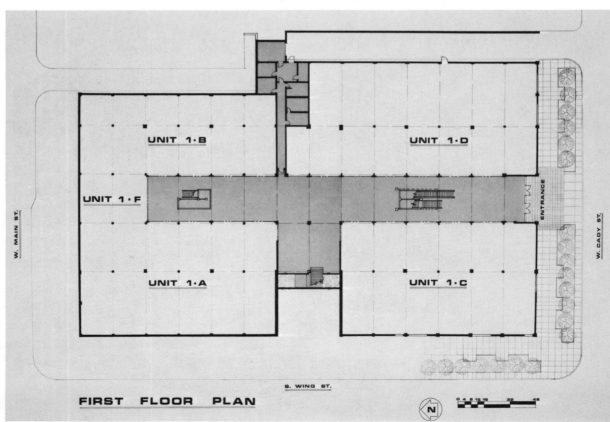

FIRST FLOOR PLAN

FISHERIES CENTER ADDITION, UNIVERSITY OF WASHINGTON

Seattle, Washington / 1969

ARCHITECT: Ralph Anderson Koch & Duarte

ARCHITECT'S COMMENTS: The form of the Fisheries Center Addition was developed in response to the limiting University of Washington campus space allotments, resulting in a rather long, narrow, multistory addition to the original older masonry and cast stone clad building. Wet laboratories were located on the lower floor, administration offices on the ground floor, and research offices and laboratories were placed on the top two floors. As a solution compatible with the structural configuration of the building and also to provide a material relating to the natural environment (with which the programs of the fisheries are so directly involved), a system of bearing masonry was selected so as to be as uniform and simple as possible with the structure doubling as finish where it occurred. Typically, each floor consists of an off-center corridor with exterior-oriented rooms on either side; the structural system follows the exterior bearing walls and one of the masonry bearing corridor partitions is connected by one-way concrete slabs. For acoustics and continuity, 6-inch nonbearing masonry was established as the other corridor partition.

The exterior walls consist of two wythes of brick with a 2-inch insulation space between, the bearing interior of 6- or 8-inch reinforced structural clay research (SCR) units and the exterior of 3-inch face units. Interior bearing partitions consist of single 6- or 8-inch wythes of reinforced SCR units or, at some lower areas, 9-inch double 4-inch wythe walls reinforced and grouted.

All efforts were pursued to achieve a uniform, homogeneous massing involving a minimum of materials. Use of steel or precast lintels and headers was avoided in lieu of developing structural members with reinforced, grout-filled masonry encasements.

(Top) South view. (Photographer: Copyright © Hugh N. Stratford)

(Bottom) East view window detail. (Photographer: Copyright © Hugh N. Stratford)

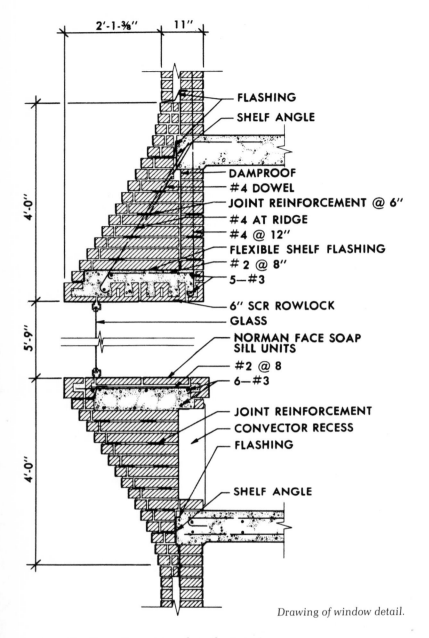

2'-1-⅜"   11"

4'-0"

5'-9"

4'-0"

FLASHING
SHELF ANGLE
DAMPROOF
#4 DOWEL
JOINT REINFORCEMENT @ 6"
#4 AT RIDGE
#4 @ 12"
FLEXIBLE SHELF FLASHING
#2 @ 8"
5—#3
6" SCR ROWLOCK
GLASS
NORMAN FACE SOAP SILL UNITS
#2 @ 8
6—#3
JOINT REINFORCEMENT
CONVECTOR RECESS
FLASHING
SHELF ANGLE

Drawing of window detail.

Further attempt to relate the interior spaces with the working environment, namely the waterway to the south of the building rather than adjacent rooftops and wall surfaces of adjacent but foreign buildings, resulted in evolving traditional brickwork detail by projecting and twisting the wall surface and focusing the windows toward the water. In constructing rotated corbeled windows, labor efficiency was maximized by the use of plywood templates. The shape of each brick course was cut from plywood, enabling each window unit to be laid up quickly and uniformly. The result, beyond the internal achievements, became a very satisfying texture of material and wall surface. Complementary detailing throughout the building provided the desired consistency and homogeneous quality.

ENGINEERING LIBRARY BUILDING, UNIVERSITY OF WASHINGTON
Seattle, Washington / 1968
ARCHITECT: **Bassetti Norton Metler**

ARCHITECT'S COMMENTS: This building is of interest in several respects. Each outside wall is different, depending upon its orientation. The south wall is almost all brick except for a couple of small windows which are hooded. The north wall is made of precast concrete panels inserted into the concrete framing with lots of glass facing northeast. However, although they are covered with brick above and below the windows, the west and east walls have a hung sunscreen about 6 or 7 feet out from the wall and about 7 feet high at one level up to about sill height to the next level above, then a clear opening for about 6 feet and then again about 7 feet high to the underside of the roof. These sunscreen panels have a honeycomb pattern made up of a special burnt clay unit which is about 8 inches deep.

East view. (Photograph: Courtesy of Bassetti Norto Metler)

KLINE SCIENCE CENTER, YALE UNIVERSITY
New Haven, Connecticut / 1975

ARCHITECT: Philip Johnson—Richard Foster
ENGINEERS: Lev Zetlin Associates

ARCHITECT'S COMMENTS: The seventeen-story tower crowns a hilltop site on the Yale campus. It provides office, classroom, library, laboratory, and clubroom space.

The walls of the tower are strongly modeled with rounded brick piers. Brownstone slabs break up the surface and reduce the size of the window openings, thus avoiding the common problem of too much light for laboratory spaces without recourse to a dull, windowless monolith.

The brick used is a dark, iron-spot brick.

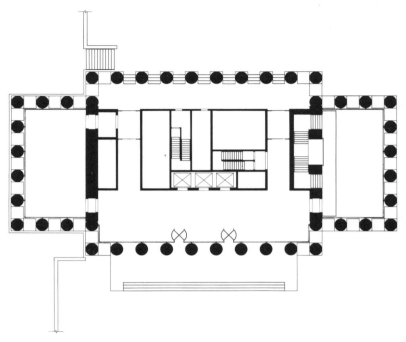

Ground floor plan.

General view. (Photographer: Copyright © Richard Payne, AIA, 1981)

Close-up view.
(Photographer: Copyright © Richard Payne, AIA, 1981)

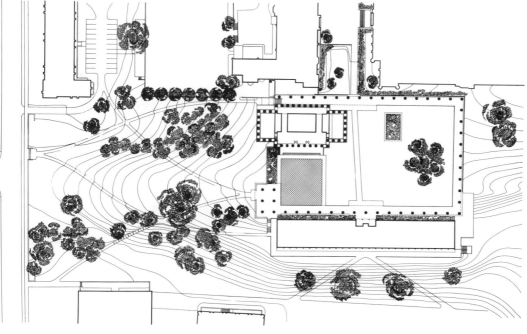

Site plan.

RESIDENTIAL COLLEGES AND ACADEMIC CORE, STATE UNIVERSITY OF NEW YORK
Amherst, New York / 1974

ARCHITECT: Davis, Brody & Associates

ARCHITECT'S COMMENTS: This educational complex for 6000 students consists of six residential colleges which cluster around an academic core and circulation spine. This spine, which connects all six colleges, forms the route along which special academic student spaces are arranged. These include libraries, teaching spaces, a drama workshop, lecture hall, and student club. The two-level spine bends around a large lawn which stretches down to an artificial lake and opens to views of the countryside beyond.

Each individual college is organized around courtyards. A paved court at the upper level connects directly to the paved plaza of the total complex. The upper court is linked to a lower, grassed courtyard at grade which leads to the surrounding meadows and athletic field. Lounges, dining facilities, and so on of each college open onto these "private" outdoor spaces.

(Top) General view. (Photographer: Norman McGrath)

(Right) Exterior view. (Photographer: Norman McGrath)

COMPUTER WAREHOUSE, STATE UNIVERSITY OF NEW YORK, UPSTATE MEDICAL CENTER

Syracuse, New York / 1970

ARCHITECT: Hueber Hares Glavin

ARCHITECT'S COMMENTS: This computer warehouse is a dual-purpose building at the large teaching hospital complex. Two unrelated functions—housing the center's computer facilities and warehousing—occupy the building. Brown split-ribbed concrete masonry units are used for the exterior and in certain areas of the interior, such as conference rooms.

Concrete masonry was selected for its ability to blend with older portions of the medical complex and for reasons of cost effectiveness.

*Exterior view.
(Photographer: Paul Norman)*

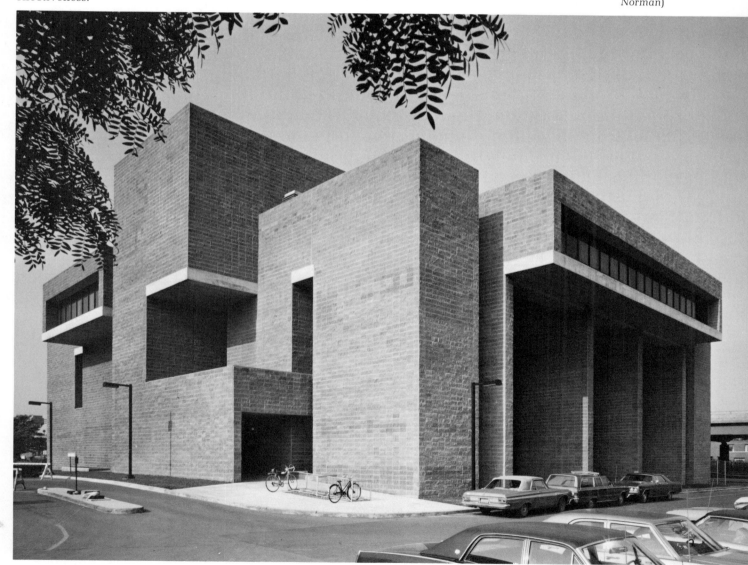

MUSIC BUILDING AND LIBRARY, EMMA WILLARD SCHOOL

Troy, New York / 1964

ARCHITECT: **Edward Larrabee Barnes, FAIA**

ARCHITECT'S COMMENTS: The library and music buildings are linked by a landscaped courtyard and enclosed corridors. Black slate roofs and bluestone exterior walls make the buildings distinctive and at the same time make them compatible with existing structures. The faculty apartments utilize a special concrete block, beige in color, for an economical match with the stone on the rest of the campus.

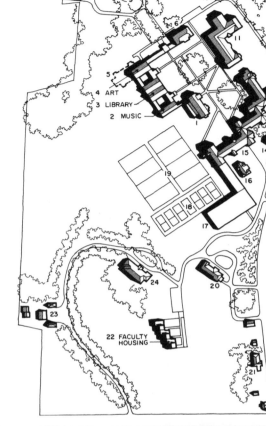

1 Chapel
2 New music building
3 New library
4 New art building
5 Existing gymnasium
6 Weaver Hall
7 Future indoor riding ring
8 Existing stable
9 Outdoor riding ring
10 New main entrance
11 Slocum Hall
12 Sage Hall
13 Undercroft
14 Power house & laundry
15 Kellas Hall
16 Northcroft
17 Future gymnasium
18 New tennis courts
19 New playing fields
20 Cluett House
21 Gorham House
22 New faculty housing
23 Service buildings
24 Wellington Lay Hall

(Right) Site plan.

(Below) Exterior view. (Photographer: Joseph Molitor)

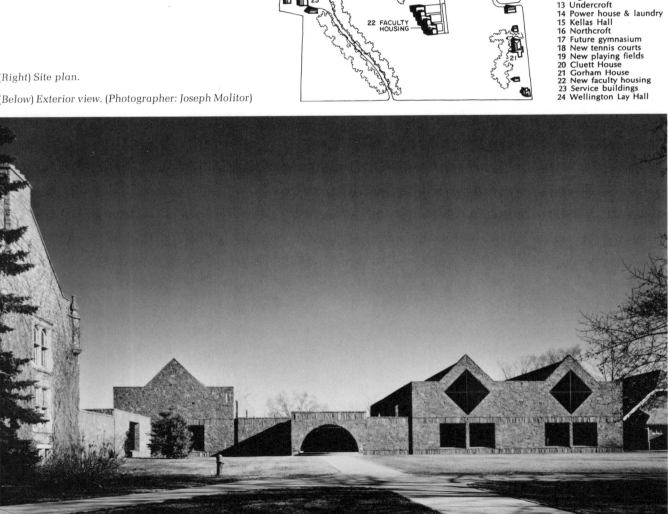

UNIVERSITY OF MASSACHUSETTS LIBRARY
Dorchester, Massachusetts / 1976

ARCHITECT: Harry Weese & Associates

ARCHITECT'S COMMENTS: Commanding a salient position on the campus of the University of Massachusetts, the Library Building relates strongly to both the community and other academic facilities which border on the Library Plaza. With vehicular access to two underlying parking levels adjoining, the main building mass has been lifted up above stepped terraces and a ceremonial ramp to the plaza, opening the view southward toward Savin Hill Cove and a grand staircase connecting the forecourt to the waterfront promenade. As an exterior room of the campus, the plaza is simply furnished with hexagonal asphalt paving blocks sloping to a single linear drain in front of steps which also serve as benches leading to a bosque of twenty-seven specimen linden trees. This simplicity extends to the library itself, with basically two materials being used, iron-spot brick and exposed unpainted concrete waffle slab on exterior soffits and interior ceilings alike. Brick is also found inside in high-use areas, with concrete block and dry wall for other partitions.

Nonlibrary functions and library service are below plaza level, with the main library areas starting with the lobby and circulation desk at one level above the plaza, reached by the circulation bridge connecting all campus buildings. A monumental stairway ascends to a mezzanine reserve collection and then on up to reference and catalogue sections. There are three typical levels over that, with double-height reading rooms flanking central multitier stack space. Library administration and outdoor reading terraces top the whole.

Main entrance. (Photographer: Jim Hedrich, Hedrich-Blessing)

(Top) Circulation desk.
(Photographer: Jim Hedrich,
Hedrich-Blessing)

(Bottom) Section.

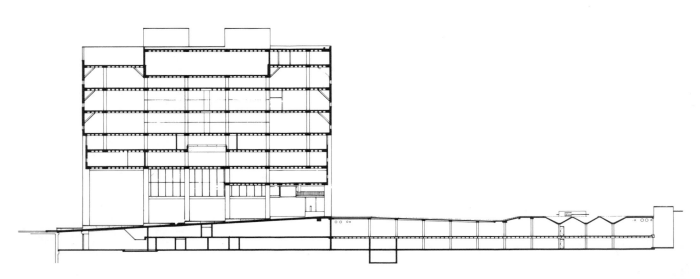

SECTION

0   5   10   20

SHELBY STATE COMMUNITY COLLEGE
Memphis, Tennessee / 1978
ARCHITECT: Walk Jones & Francis Mah, Inc.

ARCHITECT'S COMMENTS: Designed as an energy-efficient complex, utility costs have been extremely low compared with similar use facilities. The main mechanical plant areas are located centrally and have the capacity for coal usage as a primary fuel. With the growing dependence on imported fuels, this has proved to be a very definite economic bonus for the school.

The exterior of the complex is sheathed with precast brick panels and minimal amounts of glazing. Tetrahedral roof trusses are exposed at the gymnasium area to allow for reduced cubage and HVAC demand.

View of main entrance. (Photographer: Copyright © Alan Karchmer)

WINFIELD DUNN DENTAL CLINICAL BUILDING, THE UNIVERSITY OF TENNESSEE CENTER FOR THE HEALTH SCIENCES

Memphis, Tennessee / 1977

ARCHITECT: Gassner Nathan & Partners Architects Planners, Inc.

ARCHITECT'S COMMENTS: Masonry was chosen as the predominant exterior material in order to provide a sense of continuity with existing Gothic collegiate buildings on campus. An 8 inch by 8 inch brick veneer masonry unit of rich brown color gives scale and warmth to the large expanses of exterior wall. This standard unit veneers the curved forms of vertical elements with no special expense. The use of masonry contributed substantially toward meeting the restrictive budget.

(Upper) Exterior. (Photographer: O. Baitz, Inc.)

(Lower) View of terrace. (Photographer: API Photographers, Inc.)

BOWDOIN COLLEGE, VISUAL ART CENTER
Brunswick, Maine / 1979
ARCHITECT: Edward Larrabee Barnes Associates

ARCHITECT's COMMENTS: The design challenge was to preserve a path from the main campus entrance to a chapel and at the same time to relate the new building to an existing museum. The solution: The new building becomes a gateway with the path running through the ground floor. An underground link ties the new building to the museum. A water-struck, wood-fired brick was chosen for the exterior of the building. It is very close in texture and color to the brick in the adjoining museum. The walls are brick and block cavity.

(Upper) Exterior view. (Photographer: Nick Wheeler)

(Lower) Exterior view showing gateway entry. (Photographer: Nick Wheeler)

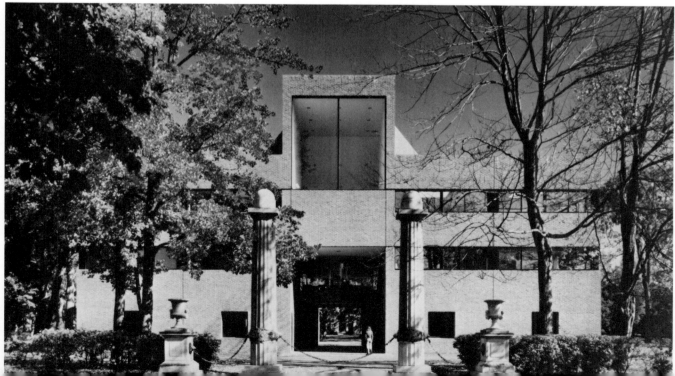

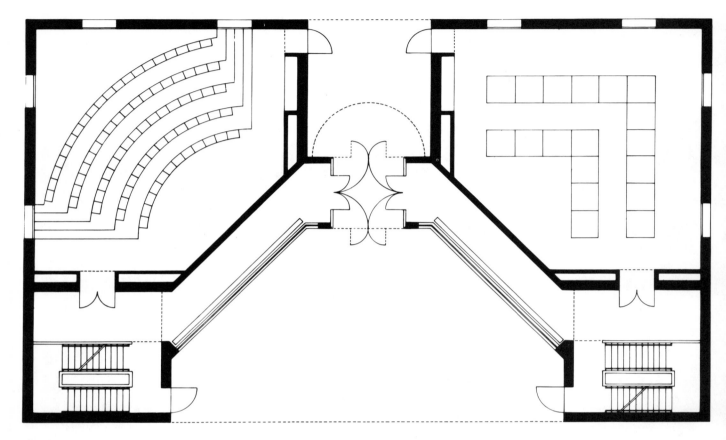

FIRST FLOOR

First floor plan.

LINDQUIST CENTER, COLLEGE OF EDUCATION, THE UNIVERSITY OF IOWA
Iowa City, Iowa / 1979
ARCHITECT: Skidmore, Owings & Merrill

ARCHITECT'S COMMENTS: This College of Education facility is designed as a two- to four-story building consisting of classrooms, class labs, learning resource center, student-faculty lounge, and office and support space for the College of Education faculty and staff. The building is divided into two zones, broadly articulated by the two-story and the four-story elements.

This building has been designed as part of a continuum begun with an earlier building. Expansion to the east is anticipated by allowing an internal connection at the second floor. Enclosed connections at the second floor to other campus buildings may be developed by bridges, to the north across College Street linking to the journalism building and on to the engineering building and to the west across Madison Street linking to the potential future construction to the south of the university library. In order to reinforce this project as a continuum, several important features of the exterior should be noted. A compatible brick blend similar to the earlier building is used. The same color glass is used in windows which repeat the design of the earlier building. The building is configured to enclose and enhance an entry plaza begun with the earlier building. This building completes a third-floor bridge, begun as part of the earlier building, and thus physically integrates the two phases.

(Left) Exterior view. (Photographer: Nick Wheeler)

(Below) Exterior view. (Photographer: Nick Wheeler)

NORTHWESTERN HIGH SCHOOL

Detroit, Michigan / 1980

ARCHITECT: Louis G. Redstone
Associates, Inc.

ARCHITECT'S COMMENTS: Accommodating 1720 students, this structure is a five-story addition to an existing performing arts theater, athletic facility, and industrial arts center. This 185,000-square-foot addition features a planetarium, mass communications center, variety of classroom types, offices, library, and counseling areas. It was completed in June 1980.

The exterior finish is brick and metal siding, selected to match the two buildings completed in earlier phases. Partitions are block, and floor finishes include quarry tile in lobby areas and stairways, terrazzo tile in corridors, and carpeting in the classrooms, planetarium, administrative offices, and library. The plaza is concrete with sculptured brick planters, forming seating arrangements under the classroom wings of the building. Window treatment is bronze insulated glass.

Because of the restricted site, it was determined that the building should be a multilevel structure. The project was also planned to be built in stages in response to the school's requirements.

(*Lower*) *Exterior view.*
(*Photographer: Daniel Bartush*)

(*Upper*) *Entrance lobby.* (*Photographer: Daniel Bartush*)

SKAGIT COUNTY ADMINISTRATION BUILDING
Mt. Vernon, Washington / 1977
ARCHITECT: The Henry Klein Partnership

ARCHITECT'S COMMENTS: This is an administration building for five county departments, a health department, and three public hearing rooms on a downtown courthouse block. The existing buildings on the limited site are a Neoclassic courthouse (1923) and a later annex (1962).

In order to complement rather than compete with the existing courthouse, the larger new administration building is separated from the courthouse and its design is informal by contrast; its height does not exceed the courthouse.

Passages through the ground level of the building are the extension of a pedestrian street and provide easy circulation from downtown, through the new building, to the old courthouse entrances beyond.

The design is a reflection of open government, providing an informal, easy access to county offices, allowing direct access from an exterior deck on the east. The serrated inner east face creates quiet alcoves for casual conferences or waiting areas for the various clinics along the length of the third floor health department.

Brick masonry was used on reinforced concrete frame or bearing brick walls.

Exterior view. (Photographer: Dick Busher)

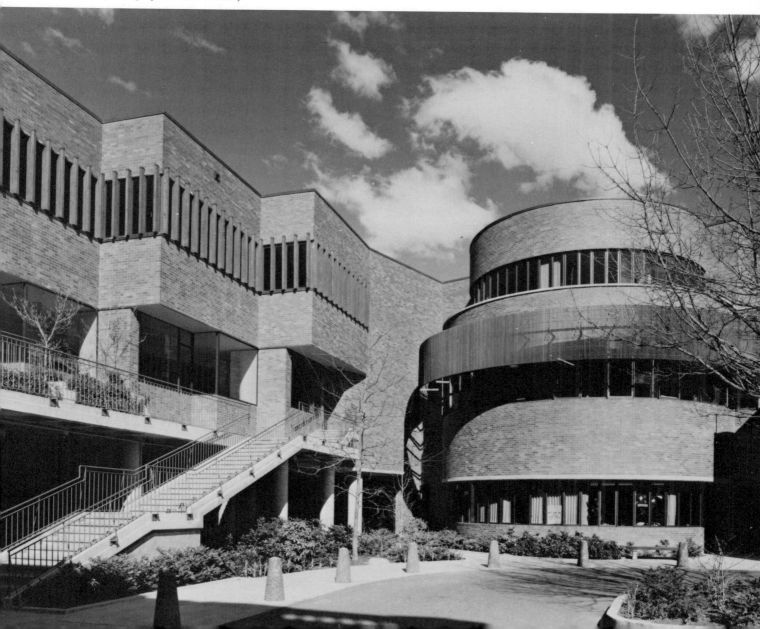

*Detail of east face.
(Photographer: Dick
Busher)*

*View from south.
(Photographer:
Copyright © Mary
Randlett)*

EAST PINE SUBSTATION
Seattle, Washington / 1967
ARCHITECT: Fred Bassetti & Company—Presently Bassetti Norton Metler Architects P.S.

ARCHITECT's COMMENTS: One of our favorite projects. It consists of an enclosure wall, a control house, and several higher walls where the main potheads are located, which needed protection from small boys throwing rocks. Bronze gates are used for viewing from the outside and also for truck access. Quite a few special shapes were used to perform various functions, as one can see in the photos. We came up with at least two very special solutions to problems we saw during the design phase.

We started out to make a double-wythe flat wall surrounding most of the project. It had to be at least 10 feet high, so it could not be single wythe, but after thinking about it I realized that if we had a dogleg brick made, it could be used for the corrugated wall. Because of the corrugation it would need to be only one brick thick and would be strong enough. But since this would have normally required a great deal of layout time on the part of the masons, we decided to make a special concrete base which would rest on a lean concrete footing and go all the way around. We did this, with a raised section alternating back and forth inside and outside of the wall with a slope to drain on each side. The bricklayers thus had merely to place the dogleg brick at each change in direction, reversing it from inside corner to outside, and all the layout was done for them. One hundred fifty or so of these precast base units were made very inexpensively since the few forms could be reused many times.

Another element of interest lies in the use of a mortar joint about 1 inch thick. This was done because on the eastern side of the project there is a major arterial running north and south. As one drives by going about 35 miles an hour a typical $\frac{1}{4}$- or $\frac{3}{8}$-inch joint would be almost invisible to the casual glance, especially the vertical joints which would be foreshortened. By making the joint much thicker than normal, the eye instantly "reads" the wall as being made up of unit masonry rather than just a typical mass of red or brown brick, which would not have had the clarity that it now has.

(Top) General view. (Photograph: Courtesy of Fred Bassetti)

(Bottom) Close-up view. (Photograph: Courtesy of Fred Bassetti)

FEDERAL BUILDING, U.S. COURTHOUSE
Fort Lauderdale, Florida / 1979
ARCHITECT: **William Morgan Architects, P.A.**

ARCHITECT's COMMENTS: Our design concept for the project called for using and expressing enduring materials. We used a concrete "tree" structural system that was exposed inside and outside consistently. For an infilling exterior panel we considered bush-hammered cast-in-place concrete and split-face concrete masonry units because of their rich textures in contrast with the smooth structural concrete bands. Masonry units finally were specified because of their cost advantage.

Special units were not required: Our design was based on standard units that would be available from several competitive sources in the vicinity of Fort Lauderdale. The units were carefully selected by the supplier before shipment and again by the contractor at the job site to assure consistent texture, size, and color.

During construction we instructed the masons to set all split-face units flush with the building's exterior surface. This resulted in a slight irregularity of block walls on their interior surfaces. The installers had to exercise care to avoid bending down the upstanding lips of interior base flashing designed to direct water from masonry voids outward. Pointing of exterior mortar joints and thorough clear waterproofing were required to complete the walls. Periodic rewaterproofing will be required at reasonable intervals to assure watertight integrity in view of the strong hurricane winds and rain in south Florida.

Court. (Photographer: Lautman Photography Washington)

Court. (*Photographer: Lautman Photography Washington*)

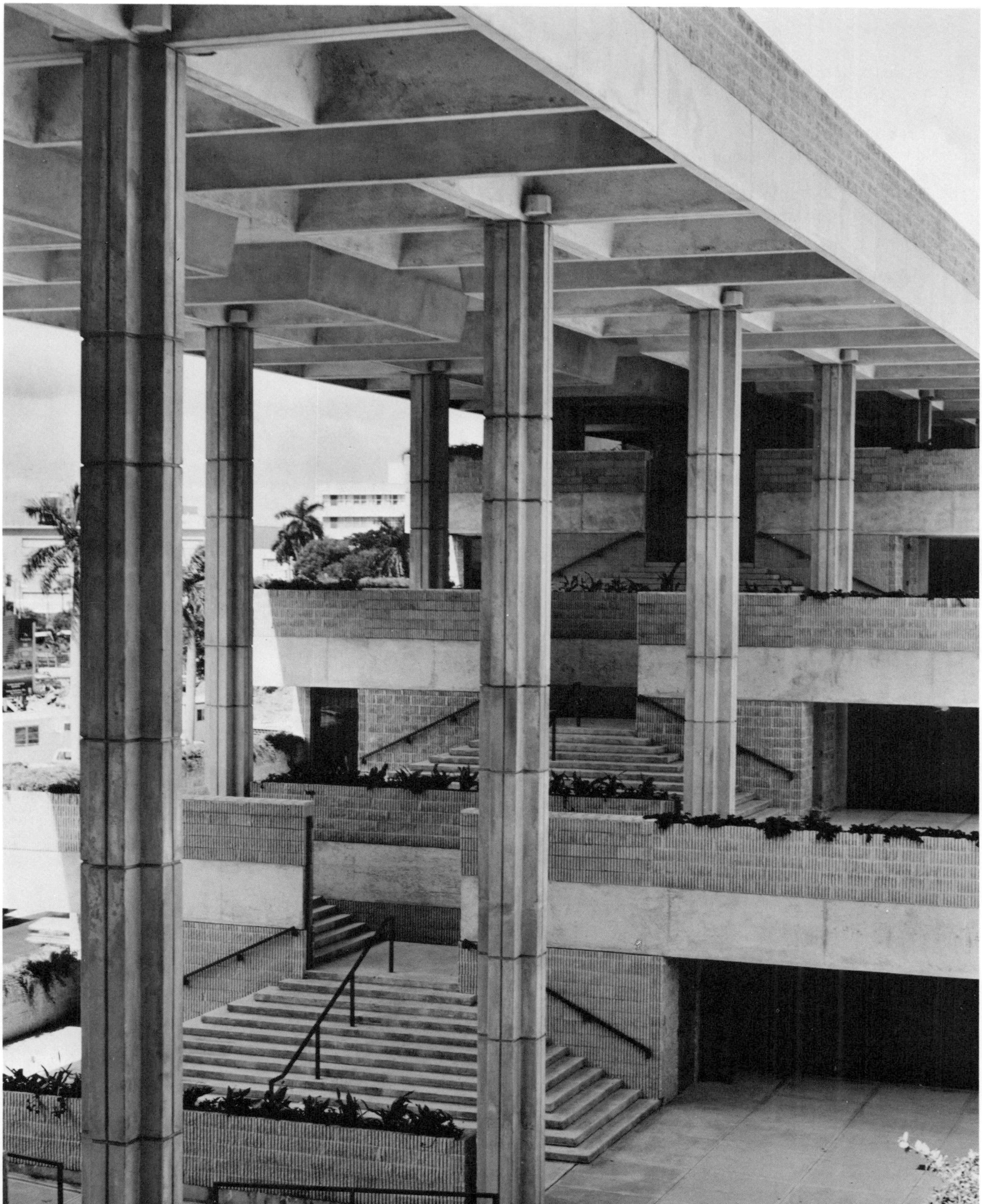

INGALLS MEMORIAL HOSPITAL PROFESSIONAL OFFICE BUILDING

Harvey, Illinois / 1977

ARCHITECT: **Perkins & Will**

ARCHITECT'S COMMENTS: The architectural challenge was to design a structure that would permit the most efficient performance, in a pleasant working environment, by the professionals utilizing the building, as well as to provide ready access to key adjacent buildings in the complex.

The exterior expression of the building was developed to be compatible with the architecture of adjacent buildings while at the same time establishing a unique expression of its own.

The brick is rawhide-toned and allows the building to blend in well with its environment.

Exterior. (Photographer: Bob Shimer, Hedrich-Blessing)

OAK BROOK VILLAGE HALL
Oak Brook, Illinois / 1976
ARCHITECT: Holabird & Root

ARCHITECT'S COMMENTS: The building is basically divided into public and private functions. Public functions are placed off a two-story galleria connecting various departments, we hope eliminating the "mazelike" character typical of many municipal buildings. The use of planting and the introduction of natural light through clerestory openings suggest an appropriate environment for the public seating areas and major stairways positioned in the space. Parking is located off both sides of the spine. The major administrative entrance is off the west side and the police entrance off the east. Security functions, such as police garages and jail cells, are located at the rear lower level of the site and are not accessible to the general public. Landscaped courts are accessible from the board room and lower level public functions. An open air "reading court" relates the existing structure to the old village hall which was to be converted to library use. The materials are brick and wood, with a concrete frame. The use of brick relates the newer building to the existing landmark structure. Soldier coursing is utilized to terminate the older building and to form radii of various sculptural elements.

(Top) Interior view. (Photograph: Courtesy of Holabird & Root)

(Bottom) Section.

Exterior view. (Photograph: Courtesy of Holabird & Root)

FORT DEARBORN STATION POST OFFICE
Chicago, Illinois / 1978
ARCHITECT: Skidmore, Owings & Merrill

ARCHITECT'S COMMENTS: The Fort Dearborn Postal Station is located on a square block site in Chicago, Illinois. It marks the first redevelopment of the Near North area. As a result, the two-story brick-clad building is set back on all four streets, the site is well landscaped, and all mail delivery vehicles, customer parking, and mail handling services are enclosed in the envelope of the building. The first level contains public service space and the loading docks. Mail sorting operations occur on the second level. Energy conservation was a prime consideration in the design. Windows open only to the north to minimize solar heat gain. High-intensity lighting is used, and most of the vehicle areas, which comprise 40 percent of the space, are naturally ventilated. The building structure is a long-span concrete waffle system exposed throughout.

(Top) Exterior view—close-up. (Photographer: Bill Engdahl, Hedrich-Blessing)

(Bottom) Exterior view. (Photograph: Courtesy of Skidmore, Owings & Merrill)

OAK PARK CIVIC CENTER

Oak Park, Illinois / 1974

ARCHITECT: Harry Weese & Associates

ARCHITECT'S COMMENTS: Oak Park has a long history of concern and respect for its architectural heritage and traditions, and the new Village Hall, as a major public building, must necessarily play a demanding role in the continuance of these traditions. The Village Hall, then, was designed as a determined marriage of both function and monument, expressed modestly in pure forms and human scale. The 70,000-square-foot facility fronts with distinctive visual impact onto a busy commercial street, while the remainder of its one-block site is given over to an open park. The central importance of the Village Hall is emphasized by its physical

(Top) Main level plan.

(Bottom) Aerial view. (Photographer: Hedrich-Blessing)

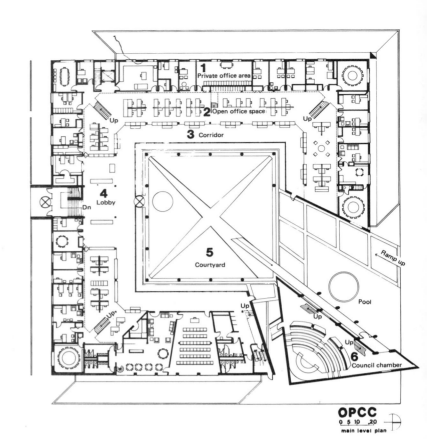

and symbolic extension into the neighborhood and vice versa.

The 140-seat council chamber is elevated above a fountain and pool and dominates the entrance to the main structure. Ramping up ceremoniously past the council chamber one enters an above-grade courtyard, symbolizing the village square, around which wrap the main portion of the building housing administrative functions and, at ground level, the police department.

Inside the hall, an "open city" government functions in landscaped open space on the ground floor and mezzanine, separated from the public only by counter units. The exposed heavy timber construction produces a warm and visually exciting environment, while the common brick exterior expresses local tradition.

(Top) View toward north. (Photographer: Jim Hedrich, Hedrich-Blessing)

(Bottom) View from north. (Photographer: Jim Hedrich, Hedrich-Blessing)

NORTH YORK MUNICIPAL BUILDING
North York, Ontario, Canada / 1978
ARCHITECT: Adamson Associates

ARCHITECT'S COMMENTS: The six-story municipal building uses the atrium space concept, with each interior floor overlooking each other, down to the lower interior pedestrian street and the cafeteria. Three glass-enclosed elevators located in the center of the building service the six office floors and parking below.

The three upper floors of the west elevations of brick-core walls accentuate the darker horizontal strips.

Interior finishes include carpeted floors, exposed sandblasted concrete columns, painted plaster perimeter walls, brick-core walls, and acoustic ceilings. All windows, balustrades, and paving are the same as the interior pedestrian street.

(Top) View of interior. (Photograph: Courtesy of Adamson Associates)

(Bottom) Exterior view—west. (Photographer: Applied Photography Ltd.)

BRICK INSTITUTE OF AMERICA
McLean, Virginia
ARCHITECT: Charles M. Goodman, FAIA

ARCHITECT'S COMMENTS: The new headquarters of the Brick Institute of America is situated on a picturesque, sloping site in McLean, Virginia, on the edge of Washington, D.C. It is composed of three discrete elements: (1) the terrace, (2) administration offices, and (3) the research foundation laboratories.

The terrace consists of a brick-surfaced platform fitted into the sloping site which forms the entrance plaza from which the administration building rises. The partially excavated space beneath this platform contains operational services, mechanical services, and utilities.

Two individual brick shafts rise from the terrace between the administration building and the research foundation laboratories. The lower height shaft contains the toilet facilities for each level. The higher contains the fire stair and elevator shaft. So placed, astride the entrance corridor and between the administration and laboratory buildings, these provide efficient vertical communication between the various parts of the complex. Their external forms, as they rise from the terrace, express these functions with simplicity and clarity.

The exhibition space is defined by four tubular shafts, each 4 feet by 8 feet in size, arranged pinwheel fashion at the corners of the space. These brick shafts rising three stories to the roof contain the mechanical and service systems which supply each floor and also provide support for beams which carry one side of the floor system of each office pavilion.

This space is in essence a three-story, galleried exhibition volume capped by a system of skylights which endow the space with changing natural light. The surrounding gallery corridors, feeding offices on three levels, provide a variety of vantage points from which to view the exhibits.

It is a dramatic environment in which to display an unlimited variety of material. Here the history of the art of brickwork can be portrayed as well as current events of significance in the progress of the art. It could be a continuously changing portrayal of the clay family in all its ramifications and its intimate association with the aspirations that human beings give form to through the architecture they evolve in their time.

(Top) Close-up view. (Photograph: Courtesy of Brick Institute of America)

(Bottom) Exterior view. (Photograph: Courtesy of Brick Institute of America)

NATIONAL SAVINGS & LOAN ASSOCIATION
Wauwatosa, Wisconsin
ARCHITECT: Py-Vavra Architects-Engineers, Inc.

ARCHITECT'S COMMENTS: The building was to be located at a prominent intersection of Mayfair Road for a sophisticated client, quite experienced in building construction and function. Therefore, the decision was made to proceed with a very positive statement in the highly successful and well-developed Mayfair area. A warm, human-scaled architecturally sculptured exterior became a goal in the design. Brick was selected early in the design process to achieve these criteria.

Additionally, brick was an ideal material, capable of adapting to the forms evolving as the design progressed for the exterior. Brick elements could be shop-fabricated where tolerances are much more easily controlled, then field-erected quite rapidly.

This construction technique was possible in large part because of the skills and talents of the masons who were holding tolerances more exacting than conventional construction so that the prefabricated elements, conventional masonry panels, and substructure would mesh together easily on the site.

(*Top*) Exterior view. (*Photograph: Courtesy of Masonry Institute of Wisconsin*)

(*Bottom*) Site plan/main floor.

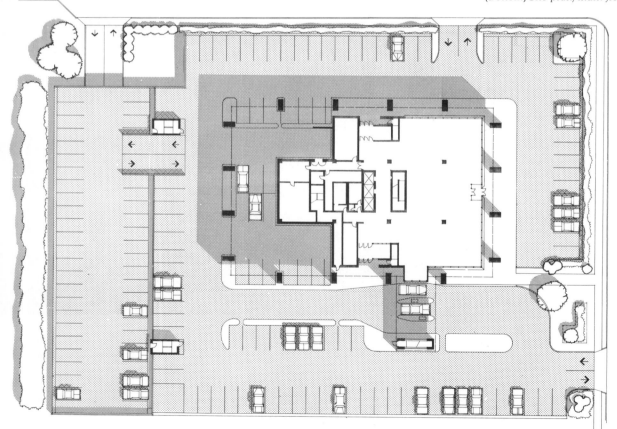

Site Plan / Main Floor   0 10 20   50

K MART INTERNATIONAL HEADQUARTERS

Troy, Michigan / 1972

ARCHITECT: Smith Hinchman & Grylls

ARCHITECT'S COMMENTS: The concept involves a complex of thirteen modular building units, each from two to four stories high, containing just over 10,000 square feet per floor. Where large uninterrupted areas are demanded, the units are connected at their faces; where offices are the prime need, units are connected at their corners, creating a number of interior courts.

Each unit is serviced by a core tower containing stairs, elevators, and all utilities and mechanical equipment. Future units, with their own service cores, can be added to a number of existing modules.

From a multistory, skylighted interior courtyard lobby, a system of diagonal pedestrian corridors connects all units at both the first and second levels, and traverses the landscaped courts.

The deep-brown earth tones of the exterior are carried through all the materials from the special size (10 inches by 16 inches) masonry blocks of all service core towers, and the building base, through the steel frame and the red-bronze tinted glass. Louvered openings in the service cores are also of specially molded, pierced masonry units.

General view. (Photographer: Balthazar Korab)

(Upper) Close-up view. (Photographer: Balthazar Korab)

(Lower) Interior court. (Photographer: Balthazar Korab)

TROY PLACE
Troy, Michigan / 1977
**ARCHITECT: Rossen/
Neuman Associates**

ARCHITECT'S COMMENTS: Exterior materials:
Double-glazed reflective glass in bronze
aluminum frames, iron-spot brick with block
back-up, Corten siding on penthouse and
garage upper level. Interior materials: Brick
paver and carpet floors, plaster, acoustical tile
and aluminum slat ceilings, vinyl-covered
dry wall with decorative formica wainscot in
corridors.

Exterior view. (Photographer: Balthazar Korab)

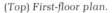

HOUSEHOLD FINANCE CORPORATE HEADQUARTERS
Northbrook, Illinois / 1978
ARCHITECT: Loebl Schlossman & Hackl

ARCHITECT'S COMMENTS: Over one million bricks were used in the construction of the Household Finance Corporate Headquarters. In addition to standard shapes, twenty-six specials were designed in response to a series of custom situations. Milliken HFC Blend brick is the principal building material used both on the exterior and the interior. Strong sculptural shapes were achieved by contrasting masonry forms with glazed areas. Concrete spandrel beams including soffits were covered with brick through the use of careful detailing of brick attachments, thus eliminating more conventionally exposed steel lintels.

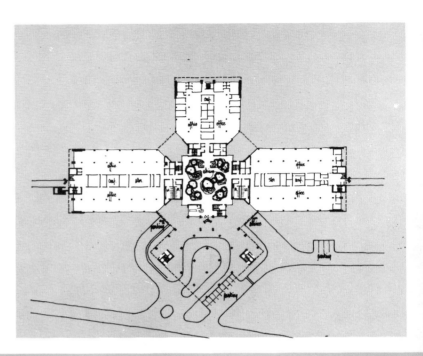

(Top) First-floor plan.

(Bottom) General view. (Photographer: Balthazar Korab)

Interior court. (Photographer: Balthazar Korab)

NORTHERN ELECTRIC COMPANY LTD.
Toronto Branch Laboratory
Bramalea, Ontario, Canada
ARCHITECT: Adamson Associates

ARCHITECT'S COMMENTS: We have no specific
problems with brick on these buildings. Our
office generally uses brick for the interior and
exterior of all buildings, as well as brick
paving, and the majority of our buildings are
in the autumn tones.

East view. (Photographer: N. & H. Studio)

SAINT LOUIS ART MUSEUM
St. Louis, Missouri

**ARCHITECT: Howard Needles
Tammen & Bergendoff**

ARCHITECT'S COMMENTS: The Saint Louis Art Museum, designed in 1904 by Cass Gilbert and expanded in 1957 by an auditorium addition on the south face, is situated on a wooded hilltop in Forest Park.

The major goal of the museum was to restore the original building and, at the same time, expand administrative and educational areas, multiuse public spaces, and storage-service areas. Decisions to devote the original building to gallery usage only and to develop new spaces for support functions provided the opportunity to express these separate functions visually in the design of the spaces.

The solution became an adjacent building that complements and contrasts with the original structure. Strong horizontal bands of glass provide contrast, while the decorative

(*Top*) *Interior showing brickwork pattern.* (*Photographer: Paul Kivett, Architectural Fotografics*)

(*Bottom*) *Exterior view.* (*Photographer: Paul Kivett, Architectural Fotografics*)

brick patterns recall the motif of the original building's Beaux Arts style.

Two types of special brick were used. In the "Dolly Parton" type, 45,000 bricks were used. The coring of these bricks had to be watched very closely. It had to be pulled back far enough not to end up outside of the $3\frac{5}{8}$-inch width in order not to be exposed to the elements.

The pattern of the brick was close to being very confusing as compared to average. This presented some problems for the masons on the job, which were solved.

There were another 95,000 special bricks used in this building.

HOLD CORE HOLES
BACK 1 3/4" MIN.

7 5/8"

3 5/8"

1 1/2"

2 1/4"

TYPE B & D

DETAIL – SPECIAL BRICK
ISOMETRIC

CUT TYPE "B" BRICK
OR FORM SEPARATE
BRICK TYPE

HOLD CORE HOLES
BACK 1 3/4" MIN.

PROFILE OF
RECESSED
STRETCHER
ALL CORE
HOLES
MUST BE
COVERED

7 5/8"

2 1/8"

1 3/4"

1/2"

2 1/4"

3 5/8"

7 5/8"

TYPE C

TYPE A

ELIMINATE CENTER
CORE OR HOLD
BACK FROM FACE
OF BRICK 1 3/4" MIN.

DETAIL – SPECIAL BRICK
ISOMETRIC

PLAN
3" : 1'-0"

Detail drawing of special brick designs.

Close-up of brickwork. (Photographer: Greg Hursley—Hursley & Lark)

THE CHARLESTON MUSEUM
Charleston, South Carolina

ARCHITECT: Crissman & Soloman
Architects Inc.

ARCHITECT'S COMMENTS: The 8 inch by 8 inch masonry unit was chosen primarily in an effort to reduce the impact of the building's size. We felt that by making the smallest scale element larger than normal we would in effect visually decrease the perceived bulk of masonry. The other major ingredient in making our selection was color. The brick chosen comes as close as any we could find to the range of color in the historic Charleston brick. Naturally because of the large quantity of brick involved, we were constrained to use a local supplier (otherwise shipping costs would have been prohibitive). The brick used is Chestnut Brown Wall Brick by Carolina Ceramics Inc., 8 inches by 8 inches by 4 inches. The floors and paving are Chestnut Brown Paver Brick by Carolina Ceramics Inc., 4 inches by 8 inches by $2\frac{1}{4}$ inches.

(Top) Exterior court. *(Photographer: Copyright © Steve Rosenthal)*

(Bottom) Exterior view. *(Photographer: Copyright © Steve Rosenthal)*

CHARLES D. WEBB WESCONNET BRANCH LIBRARY
Jacksonville, Florida / 1979

ARCHITECT: **Pappas Associates Architects, Inc.**

ARCHITECT'S COMMENTS: Located on a major street, the library is positioned on an elevated plane to give the building dominance over the site. The key feature of the south-facing main facade is an arched portico of light buff-colored brick. The portico serves as a sunscreen for the glass wall behind, shading the interior from the hot Florida sun in a construction form that goes back to the early Spanish settlers of the state. The portico was articulated to allow the sun to cast everchanging patterns on its face. This effect is achieved by corbeled radial bands, in which projecting brick accentuates each band.

Although the library proper is steel frame construction, the arches in the portico are load-bearing.

(Top) Site plan.

(Bottom) General view. *(Photograph: Courtesy of Pappas Associates Architects, Inc.)*

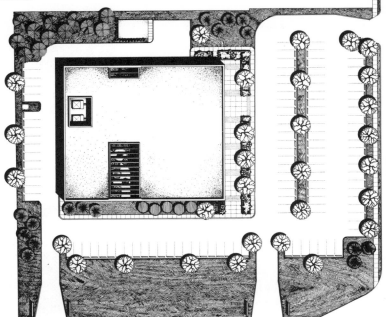

Harlow Boulevard

SITE PLAN

Close-up view of brickwork. (Photograph: Courtesy of Pappas Associates Architects, Inc.)

CHILDREN'S ZOO
Seattle, Washington / 1967

**ARCHITECT: Fred Bassetti & Company—
Presently Bassetti Norton Metler
Architects P.S.**

ARCHITECT'S COMMENTS: The item of interest here is the serpentine wall which surrounds the whole children's zoo and is made up of brick put together in an open work pattern. The serpentine wall was used because this makes possible construction with a single wythe of brick, as Thomas Jefferson did so long ago at the University of Virginia. A special quality of this wall is that the bricks are separated, the vertical joints being about 2 or 3 inches apart with an open space at that point. This creates a feeling of openness through the wall. It will be noticed that at the bottom and at two levels in between the open work disappears and bricks are placed in a normal running bond. This is because in the horizontal center joint of these three courses there is a "K" web for stiffening. It seems strange that the engineer required that we use this because I would have thought the enhanced strength of a serpentine wall would have been enough. There are some special features in addition, such as the serrated top of the wall. Also where the grade changes level, the wall steps down one or two courses at a time and there's a special provision made for that, as can be seen in the photographs.

(*Top*) *General view.* (*Photographer: Art Hupy*)

(*Bottom*) *General view.* (*Photographer: Hugh N. Stratford*)

GERMANTOWN MUNICIPAL CENTER
Germantown, Tennessee
ARCHITECT: McGehee Nicholson Burke Architects Inc.

ARCHITECT'S COMMENTS: We have used specially shaped brick for some time with good results and cooperation from the supplier and the manufacturer. We are finding recently, however, some reluctance by manufacturers to produce the special shapes. The special shapes on the Germantown project were detailed on the construction drawings and were priced accordingly as the project was bid. The manufacturer of the brick furnished full-size details of the brick and requested some minor changes in the special shapes to better suit the manufacturing techniques.

A sand face brick was selected in lieu of a wire cut because these were the only textures available without extensive and costly hand molding. Delivery of the special shapes requires an additional four weeks minimum after approval of shop drawings.

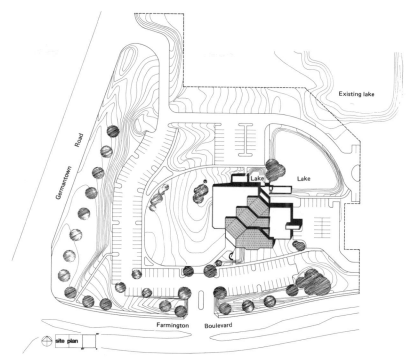

(Top) Site plan.

(Bottom) Exterior, east view. (Photographer: Copyright © Alan Karchmer)

Plan at wall.

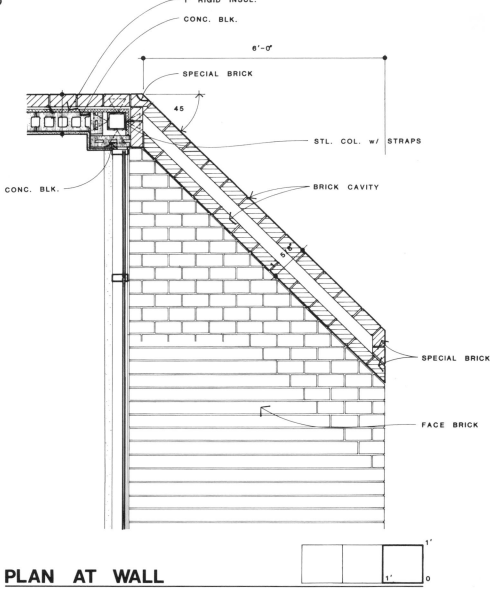

1" RIGID INSUL.

CONC. BLK.

SPECIAL BRICK

6'-0"

45

STL. COL. w/ STRAPS

BRICK CAVITY

CONC. BLK.

SPECIAL BRICK

FACE BRICK

PLAN AT WALL

1'

1'   0

Close-up of brickwork. (Photographer: James L. Burke, Jr.)

COLEMAN A. YOUNG RECREATION CENTER
Detroit, Michigan / 1980
ARCHITECT: William Kessler & Associates, Inc.

ARCHITECT'S COMMENTS: The building was designed using a 24-foot bay size which was subdivided into numerous vertical and horizontal planning grids with the lowest common denominator being 8 inches.

A durable low-cost interior and exterior material was required. We selected an 8 inch by 16 inch center-scored ground-faced masonry unit which is polished to a warm gray terrazzolike finish. The masonry module established an 8 inch by 8 inch grid, giving the appearance that not one block is cut to construct the facility. This uninterrupted grid continues with the use of 8 inch by 8 inch glass block as a glazing material, chosen because of its durability and ease of replacement.

The use of the neutral colors of gray masonry and glass block were enlivened with one green accent color throughout the project which unified the architecture into an inviting, dynamic environment.

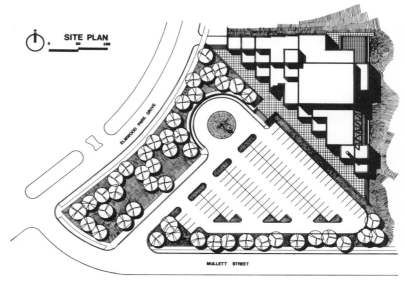

(Top) Site plan.

(Bottom) General view. (Photograph: Courtesy of William Kessler.)

Close-up view. (Photographer: Balthazar Korab)

CITADEL THEATRE
Edmonton, Alberta, Canada / 1976

ARCHITECT: Diamond, Myers, & Wilkin
DESIGN: Barton Myers and R. L. Wilkin, Partners-in-Charge
IMPLEMENTATION: Barton Myers Associates and R. L. Wilkin Architects

ARCHITECT'S COMMENTS*: Throughout the building, basic building construction elements are raised to the level of finished materials. This means that for brick, structural steel, concrete, steel deck, concrete block, ductwork and sprinklers, the work quality must be of the highest standard, and the detailing must, while respecting the economics and fabrication integrity of "off the shelf" elements, seek to combine and juxtapose these elements in an elegant and mutually supportive manner. The basic building material is a pressed red brick from Medicine Hat, Alberta. This brick was traditionally used in the construction of Edmonton buildings. However today, except for a few notable older buildings, the theater's brick is the exception among its present precast concrete neighbors. In addition to being a reinstatement of an excellent regional building material, the brick selected also evokes the old brick Salvation Army citadel, in which the theater was founded, and provides some of the warmth in color and texture the client was seeking. The brick is used both for exterior rain screen cladding and for the interior walls around the main theater and along the pedestrian mall. It is complemented by unglazed red clay tile floors in the pedestrian mall and under the skylight area in the upper lobby. The aluminum sash curtain wall and skylights, the porcelain enameled steel insulated panels, and the structural steel supporting these elements, while clearly understood as front of house elements, are also identified with the building as a whole by being painted or enameled to match the brick.

*Reprinted with permission of *The Canadian Architect*, July, 1977, p. 22.

(Right) Birds-eye view of theater looking east. (Photographer: John Fulker, John Fulker & Associates Ltd.)

(Below) Exterior view — close-up. (Photographer: John Fulker, John Fulker & Associates Ltd.)

BURNS CLINIC MEDICAL CENTER, P.C. NORTHERN MICHIGAN HOSPITALS, INC.

Petoskey, Michigan / 1978

ARCHITECT: Graheck, Bell, Kline & Brown, Inc.—James Falick/The Klein Partnership

ARCHITECT'S COMMENTS: The project consisted of additions to two existing buildings in the hospital-medical complex. The four-level clinic addition provides 52,000 square feet and was completed in 1978. The hospital addition, completed the following year, provides 185,000 square feet on five levels. The buildings are of a unified design in brick masonry. Design features of both buildings include continuous windows with sloping brick sills at spandrel sections, and curbed brick columns and stair towers. The usage of brick is carried into the lobby areas of both buildings.

Exterior view. (Photographer: Balthazar Korab)

RIVER DISTRICT HOSPITAL

**St. Clair Shores,
Michigan / 1977**

ARCHITECT: **Louis G. Redstone
Associates, Inc.**

ARCHITECT'S COMMENTS: The design decision was to build the addition at the front of the existing structure rather than behind it. Because of the unusually long and narrow site, this concept met both functional and aesthetic objectives. It covered and updated the outward appearance image of the hospital, making it visible and identifiable from a distance. And it fulfilled the goal of increasing the hospital's outpatient orientation by making outpatient services directly accessible to the public.

Also an entrance canopy instead of a vestibule was decided upon. This provides protection, yet allows natural lighting for outdoor planters, with an unobstructed view from inside the reception area.

The exterior finish, 8 inch by 8 inch extruded brick, was chosen for its visual appearance and surface texture. The combination of flat and fluted textures related particularly well to the window openings.

Exterior view. (Photographer: Balthazar Korab)

ISHAM HUMAN AND COMMUNITY DEVELOPMENT CENTER
YMCA OF METROPOLITAN CHICAGO
Chicago, Illinois / 1981
ARCHITECT: **Metz Train Youngren**

ARCHITECT'S COMMENTS: Exterior glazed bricks
define functional areas and provide low
maintenance, with color usage continued on
interior mechanical ducts against high-glass
white walls. The articulated roofline houses
the mechanical systems, and the linear
design provides maximum security control.
The exterior glazed bricks are laid in strips of
ten colors.

(Top) Exterior view. (Photographer: John Hilarides)

(Bottom) Close-up of brick detail. (Photographer: John Hilarides)

ARVADA CENTER FOR THE ARTS AND HUMANITIES
Community Center, Arvada, Colorado / 1976

**ARCHITECT: Perkins & Will in association with
Seracuse, Lawler & Partners**

COMMENTS BY C. WILLIAM BRUBAKER, EXECUTIVE
VICE PRESIDENT OF PERKINS & WILL, INC: Brick
was chosen because it is the basic, traditional
"Denver material." It was used in the
amphitheater as well as in the building itself.

For this low-rise building with a number of
windowless walls (such as those enclosing the
theater), brick was the logical material for
good energy conservation qualities, for
economy and ease of construction, and for
the desired design quality.

The octagonal building forms, which create
a distinctive skyline, were conceived with
brick in mind.

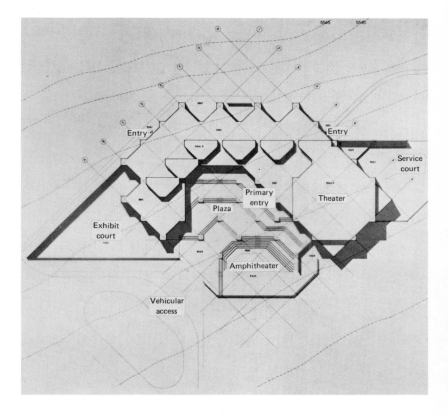

(*Top*) *Roof plan.*

(*Bottom*) *Exterior view.* (*Photographer: Uptown
Photography, Inc., Denver; Jim Krebs, Photographer*)

BOSTON CITY HOSPITAL OUTPATIENT DEPARTMENT BUILDING

Boston, Massachusetts / 1977

ARCHITECT: **Hugh Stubbins & Associates, Inc.**

The building is an air-rights structure spanning Massachusetts Avenue, one of Boston's major arteries and linking nurses' and interns' housing to the south of the avenue with the future fifteen-story inpatient building on the north side. It provides for twenty-two waiting rooms divided among the five floors of the building. Each clinic floor is similar in design to that of an airline terminal with small waiting rooms aligned along the perimeter corridors.

(Top) Section through intake and exhaust plenum.

(Bottom) Plaza showing brick enclosure around the mechanical intakes. (Photographer: Copyright © Edward Jacoby—Architectural Photography Group)

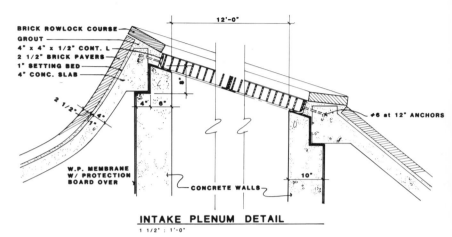

BRICK ROWLOCK COURSE
GROUT
4" x 4" x 1/2" CONT. L
2 1/2" BRICK PAVERS
1" SETTING BED
4" CONC. SLAB

W.P. MEMBRANE W/ PROTECTION BOARD OVER

CONCRETE WALLS

12'-0"

#6 at 12" ANCHORS

10"

INTAKE PLENUM DETAIL
1 1/2" : 1'-0"

ST. PROCOPIUS ABBEY CHURCH AND MONASTERY

Lisle, Illinois / 1972

ARCHITECT: Loebl Schlossman & Hackl

ARCHITECT'S COMMENTS: The entire St. Procopius complex was constructed in common brick. Predominate use of common brick and other natural materials served to heighten the quality of the complex's architectural space.

In addition to standard shapes, twenty-six specials were designed in response to a series of custom situations. Milliken HFC Blend brick is the principal building material used both on the exterior and the interior. Strong sculptural shapes were achieved by contrasting masonry forms with glazed areas. Concrete spandrel beams were covered with brick attachments, thus eliminating more conventionally exposed steel lintels.

(Top) Bell tower. (Photographer: Copyright © Philip A. Turner)

(Bottom) Exterior view. (Photographer: Copyright © Philip A. Turner)

ST. PROCOPIUS (Cont.)

(Top) Main level floor plan.

(Bottom) Interior view. (Photographer: Balthazar Korab)

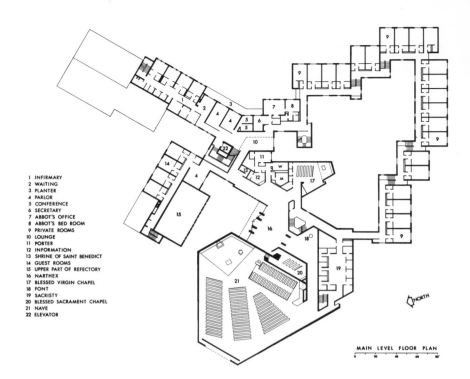

1 INFIRMARY
2 WAITING
3 PLANTER
4 PARLOR
5 CONFERENCE
6 SECRETARY
7 ABBOT'S OFFICE
8 ABBOT'S BED ROOM
9 PRIVATE ROOMS
10 LOUNGE
11 PORTER
12 INFORMATION
13 SHRINE OF SAINT BENEDICT
14 GUEST ROOMS
15 UPPER PART OF REFECTORY
16 NARTHEX
17 BLESSED VIRGIN CHAPEL
18 FONT
19 SACRISTY
20 BLESSED SACRAMENT CHAPEL
21 NAVE
22 ELEVATOR

MAIN LEVEL FLOOR PLAN

CHURCH OF THE RESURRECTION
Memphis, Tennessee
ARCHITECT: Taylor & Crump Architects, Inc.

ARCHITECT'S COMMENTS: The concept was to create a building with a maximum degree of sculptural power because the Church of the Resurrection wished to announce and to identify its presence in the neighborhood in a very strong, permanent way.

The specific building forms evolved primarily from a consideration of the interior uses of the building and the types of spaces needed to house them as well as a desire for geometric strength and simplicity.

Although a number of exterior materials were considered, brick was chosen for a number of reasons: durability, economy, availability, color-fastness, ease of adaptation to a variety of building forms and details, and surface texture.

(*Top*) Floor plan.

(*Center*) Section.

(*Bottom*) Exterior view showing chapel. (*Photographer: Bemis Atkins*)

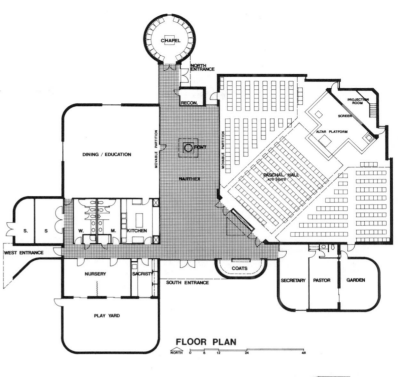

FLOOR PLAN

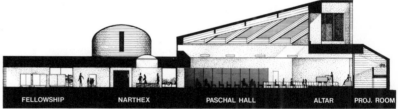

FELLOWSHIP   NARTHEX   PASCHAL HALL   ALTAR   PROJ. ROOM

TEMPLE ISRAEL
Memphis, Tennessee / 1976

ARCHITECT: Gassner Nathan & Partners
CONSULTING ARCHITECT: Percival Goodman

(*Upper*) *Exterior view.*
(*Photographer: O. Baitz, Inc.*)

(*Lower*) *Outer lobby.*
(*Photographer: O. Baitz, Inc.*)

ARCHITECT'S COMMENTS: The focal point of the complex is the sanctuary, a semicircular, skylit space accommodating 1335 people. The sanctuary is entered as a climax from a progression of spaces starting with a glass-covered entrance garden, a two-storied reception area, and a more intimate memorial foyer. The semicircular, theater type of plan allows all congregants to be within fifteen rows of the ark. This, along with the extensive use of wood and stained glass, achieves the desired feeling of intimacy. At the same level as the sanctuary balcony is a gallery for archives and exhibits of Judaica.

The basic structure is steel with masonry used extensively on the interior as well as the exterior. There are oak ceilings in the sanctuary, chapel, and entrance foyer. Oak is also used for paneling, trim, and doors. Other materials are carpeted floors, vinyl-covered gypsum board walls, and acoustic ceilings. The structure has been designed for seismic zone 3.

Special attention was given to an overall program of art works. Tapestries, stained glass, mosaics, and most ritual objects were designed and executed by the artist-designer working closely with the architect and building committee.

HILLTOP APARTMENTS
Selah, Washington / 1979

ARCHITECT: Knipper Dunn Partnership

(Upper) Site plan.

(Lower) General view. (Photographer: Copyright © Mary Randlett, 1982)

ARCHITECT'S COMMENTS: The client and the architect resolved at the onset that the pursuance of low maintenance, energy savings, and a quality environment to complement the unique site would be the major goals of the project. It was also determined that the design should accommodate future conversion from apartments to condominiums. Because of the economic considerations of the project, these goals would have to be realized within the confines of a moderately low budget.

The site was impressive. Winding along the undulating brow of a knoll in the high foothills it sat like an eagle's nest overlooking the valley below. But, as beautiful as this natural area was, it was not without it's architectural drawbacks. Ingress and egress were limited to one finite location. An existing 12-foot-diameter water tank 36 feet high had to be incorporated into the design. An irrigation canal that formed the south, east, and west boundaries of the site severely limited the location of buildings and drain fields. Balancing the desired number of units with the parking requirements, the circulation requirements, and the other site and economical limitations was an ongoing architectural juggling act before the final plan was evolved.

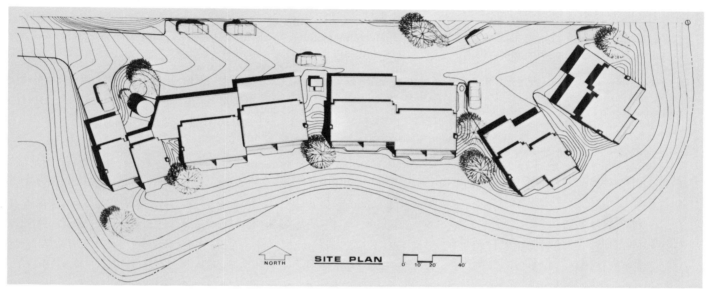

SITE PLAN

Of interest to the reader are the energy saving measures used in the total design concept. These have resulted in saving more than half of the Department of Energy's (DOE) proposed energy conservation budget recommendation of 100,000 Btu's.

Energy-Saving Measures

- Use of concrete slab and concrete block wall mass for energy retention.
- Concrete block is insulated at exterior walls and sand-filled for sound at common interior walls.
- Solar screen design lets in the low warming rays of the winter sun, while cutting off the heat of the high summer sun to cool the living spaces.
- Earth sheltered by setting building into hillside and berming sidewalls.
- Liberal use of common sidewalls within design parameters.
- Location of carport and knoll behind, as well as the units being recessed into the hillside, helps to protect the units from prevailing winter winds.
- The attached carport also provides shade in the summer and some heat retention in the winter for the north wall of the unit.
- The concrete floor slabs of the kitchen, dining and living room are warmed by the winter sun.
- Light-colored patio slab reflects light and heat into units through south-facing glazed area in winter; is cut off by sunscreen in summer.
- Ninety-two percent of the unit's window area faces south for maximum solar efficiency.
- The remaining 8 percent of the window area provides through ventilation for the upper and lower floors and natural light for the stairs and bath.
- The near cube shape of each unit optimizes the volume/surface exposure ratio for least heat loss potential.
- Secondary use rooms occur along the north wall, insulating and providing more comfortable primary living areas.
- Patio sidewalls give visual and sound privacy, act as windbreaks, and radiate warmth as the evening cools.
- Added solar control is provided by 1-inch slat-type blinds on all glass.
- Furniture located on interior walls requires less energy to maintain comfort.
- Units are provided with chimneys for wood stoves or free-standing fireplaces for possible future installation.

Close-up view. (Photographer: Copyright © Mary Randlett, 1982)

WATERSIDE APARTMENTS
New York, New York / 1974
ARCHITECT: Davis, Brody & Associates

ARCHITECT'S COMMENTS: The most northern of the four towers at Waterside is thirty-one floors high, with twelve apartments per floor. By constricting itself to tall, narrow towers, it opens the river view as much as possible. The bricks developed for this project were $5\frac{1}{2}$ inches by 8 inches and 8 inches by 8 inches.

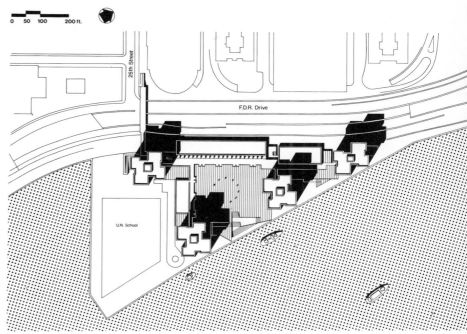

(Top) Site plan.

(Bottom) View from East River. (Photographer: Robert Gray)

Exterior view. (Photographer: Robert Gray)

GHENT SQUARE TOWNHOUSES
Norfolk, Virginia / 1979
ARCHITECT: Barton Myers Associates

ARCHITECT'S COMMENTS: Ghent Square is part of an urban renewal project for a residential area near downtown Norfolk, Virginia. The area had been razed and a new infrastructure installed, incorporating a series of parks culminating in a major square which houses an old ferry terminal building recycled as a community center. The plan, developed by the Norfolk Redevelopment and Housing Authority, echoes the pattern of open space development of old residential Norfolk, which resembles the well-known example of Savannah.

The predominant element of this design is the combined bay window chimney. These two elements, which are often emphasized independently in residential architecture, particularly in Virginia, are combined here as a major feature of the facade of the square. Elements such as working exterior shutters, balconies, and brick and wood construction materials reinforce the traditional aspects of the design. The Flemish bond brickwork, also in character with the neighborhood, adds a distinctive pattern to the brick walls.

(*Left*) Exterior view. (*Photographer: Lautman Photography*)

(*Below*) Site plan.

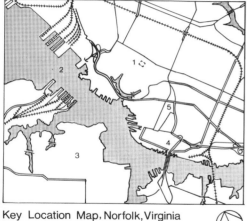

1 Ghent Square
2 Elizabeth River
3 City of Portsmouth
4 Civic Centre
5 Convention Centre

Key Location Map, Norfolk, Virginia
0   1 mile

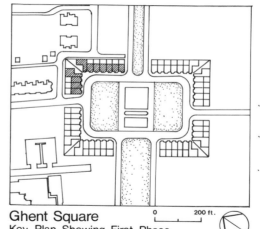

Ghent Square
Key Plan Showing First Phase
0   200 ft.

PARCEL 30

Type A -
`The Town House`

Type B -
`The Corner House`

Type C -
`The Court House`

CHAPTER THREE

Foreign Countries

This chapter includes projects from a number of countries of diverse cultures and religions. Some are located in highly industrialized countries; others are in emerging ones.

It is interesting to note that excellent skill in masonry is part of the tradition and history of countries such as England, Italy, and Spain. Present-day architects continue the tradition by utilizing advanced technical systems in their various design concepts.

In the developing countries, the annual Aga Khan Award, established in 1977, has stimulated and encouraged the Muslim cultural tradition to utilize modern technology. In establishing this award, the Aga Khan commented: "I have become increasingly concerned with the physical form that the Islamic world will take in the future: the houses we live in, our places of work, the institutions that serve us, the gardens and parks where we rest, the markets and, of course, the mosques."

There are many excellent examples of significant masonry projects to be found on nearly every continent. However, due to space limitations, only a few could be presented here. It is my intention to highlight the wide range of interesting design concepts to which this material can be so well adapted.

HALAWA HOUSE
Agamy,
Egypt / 1975

ARCHITECT: Abdel
Wahed El-Wakil
STONE MASON:
Aladdin Mustapha

ARCHITECT'S COMMENTS: This two-story
single-family summer home near Alexandria,
completed in 1975, makes use of Egyptian
archetypes, alcoves, belvederes, wind
catchers, vaults, and domes. Cited for design
and construction of a house which represents
a dedicated search for identity with
traditional forms, it was built with limestone
walls and sandstone floors.

Aladdin Mustapha, 76, an Egyptian master
mason, shared the Aga Khan Award for
Architecture with the architect Abdul Wahed
El Wakil for his skill in erecting this home.

(Upper) Summer home—construction of arch. (Photograph: Courtesy of Abdel
Wahed El-Wakil—The Aga Khan Award for Architecture)

(Lower) Summer home—forming of the arches. (Photograph: Courtesy of
UNESCO—The Aga Khan Award for Architecture)

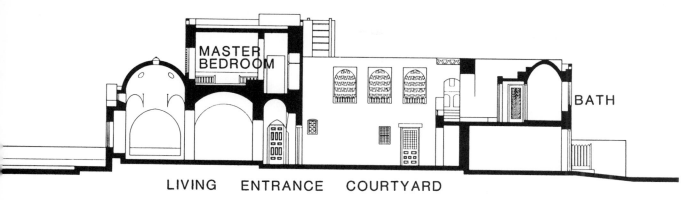

MASTER BEDROOM

BATH

LIVING ENTRANCE COURTYARD

(Upper) Summer home—section. (Photographer: C. Avedissian—The Aga Khan Award for Architecture)

(Lower) Summer home. (Photographer: Copyright © Christopher Little—The Aga Khan Award for Architecture)

LOUDOUN ROAD BUILDINGS
**Camden (London),
England / 1980**

ARCHITECT: **Tom Kay Associates**

ARCHITECT'S COMMENTS: One type contains 11,000 square feet of ground-level workshops, replacing industrial space demolished in the redevelopment area. Twenty-six units are three- and four-person residential units. The density is 132 persons per acre in addition to the commercial coverage of the land.

The other type contains six shops, two flats for shopkeepers, and twelve craft rooms or studios, replacing similar types of space demolished in the redevelopment area.

The two buildings form a "gateway" into a large council-designed redevelopment area including housing and schools and are virtually the last two buildings in a very prolonged project.

Although only completed in 1980, initial scheme designs for the two sites were prepared in the mid-1970s at a time when it seemed likely that the brick industry would gradually change over to a metric modular format. The brick chosen was 200 millimeters by 100 millimeters by 100 millimeters. Since then it has become apparent that architects are reluctant to make this change, and the metric modular ranges are being withdrawn from production.

The buildings employ a number of special bricks, including double-sized capping bricks. On vulnerable corners, a number of shaped precast concrete blocks have been used (where shear weight is an advantage in resisting accidental damage and frost heave).

Both buildings are a mixture of load-bearing masonry and reinforced concrete framed construction. It was a conscious decision not to express these different methods. Hence brick was used overall, both structurally and as a facing.

(Below) Exterior view showing type II building. (Photographer: Tom Kay)

(Opposite) Exterior of type I building. (Photographer: Tom Kay)

WEST HILL PARK
Highgate, (London)
England / 1976
ARCHITECT: Ted Levy
Benjamin & Partners

ARCHITECT'S COMMENTS*: The client asked for a high-quality, village-type development with a variety of house types and accommodation, but with flexibility in the planning.

The sizes of units range from one-bedroom studios to four-bedroom detached houses, but there is also a modest block of flats with two large penthouses. We set out to achieve an architectural effect in harmony with the surroundings.

The houses and garden walls are constructed of rich handmade Dorking bricks with handmade specials for sills, copings, and so on. The second phase is in Conyer Sheppey bricks similar to old London stock, both by Redland Bricks.

The special handmade bricks are of the same modular size as the ordinary brick in the majority of cases but are chamfered and shaped to suit the particular location, such as double-chamfered when used as coping bricks, single-chamfered when used as sill bricks, single-chamfered when used as lintels. In addition, however, where used as copings, the special bricks are of double size and used as corner returns.

The bricks are of the same material as the facing bricks but baked separately so that they show a slight variation in color. The laying and mortar joints and pointing are of the same method and material as the ordinary bricks.

The cost of the special bricks is approximately twice that of ordinary bricks, but no special problems were encountered with these since they are of the same material as ordinary bricks.

*Excerpted from *Architect's Journal*, London, England, October 13, 1976.

(Upper) View of terrace. (Photographer: Horst Kolo)
(Lower) Side view. (Photographer: Copyright © Sam Lambert)

(Upper) Exterior view. (Photograph: Courtesy of Malcolm Hecks Associates)

(Lower) Close-up view. (Photograph: Courtesy of Malcolm Hecks Associates)

EUROPA HOUSE, BRITISH AIRWAYS OFFICES
Heathrow Airport, Cranford,
Middlesex, England

ARCHITECT: Malcolm Hecks Associates

STROUDWATER PARK FLATS
Weybridge, Surrey, England
ARCHITECT: Malcolm Hecks Associates

(Top) Close-up view. (Photograph:
Courtesy of Malcolm Hecks Associates)

(Bottom) General exterior view.
(Photograph: Courtesy of Malcolm Hecks
Associates)

MAIDENHEAD LIBRARY
Berkshire, England / 1972
ARCHITECT: Ahrends Burton & Koralek, Architects

ARCHITECT'S COMMENTS: A square plan on three levels was developed. The ground level provided for the main lending library, children's library, music library, and exhibition space. The upper level was designed as part of the whole space but sufficiently separate for quiet and privacy, and reference and study sections and meeting rooms. Below, in a semibasement taking advantage of the steep slope of the site down to the stream, are the book stacks, administration and staff rooms, and provision for a mobile library service.

The roof is a clear-span space frame which was constructed on the ground and jacked up into position where it is supported independently from the rest of the structure by eight cruciform reinforced concrete columns. A secondary structure supports the mezzanine gallery inside. Large bay window elements, their tops splayed at the same angle as the space frame overhang above, contribute to the profile of the interior space by providing protected alcoves for a variety of functions and are also principal modulating elements on the exterior.

It became a building with two scales: the large scale of the roof as a simple square enclosure sheltering and giving unity to the whole volume below, floating over a village of small-scale varied spaces created by the brick structures below.

(Top) Exterior view. (Photographer: John Donat Photography)
(Bottom left) Close-up exterior view. (Photographer: John Donat Photography)
(Bottom right) Interior view. (Photographer: John Donat Photography)

FIRE SERVICE HEADQUARTERS
**Greater Manchester County,
Swinton, England / 1980**

ARCHITECT: **Building Design Partnership**

ARCHITECT'S COMMENTS*: The Greater Manchester Council (GMC) County Fire Service wished to develop its existing suburban site as a new control center, offices for senior personnel, and central stores. The GMC Fire Service is the third largest in Great Britain and is responsible for an area of about 500 square miles, with a population of 2.7 million. There are 41 fire stations with 104 appliances. About 50,000 calls are handled each year by a staff of 2293

*Excerpted from *The Architect's Journal*, London, England, September 17, 1980, pp. 546–548.

operational fire fighters, 82 control staff, and 300 civilian staff. The site, on the A666 trunk road between Manchester and Swinton, consisted of a Victorian house (Shade House) and a two- to three-story speculative office block which had recently been acquired and converted to headquarters accommodation. The Victorian house was demolished in March 1976 to make way for the new proposals. The site is very restricted in area, approximately 4300 square meters, and is surrounded by semidetached housing. The form of design emerged from two main influences: First, development was initially considered to be phased, with stores, offices, control center, and caretaker's flat to be built sequentially (but actually built simultaneously); second, the site is on a noisy trunk road. Efforts have therefore been made, in consultation with the planning authority, to screen out the road, to reduce the apparent scale of the buildings, and to use materials

(*Top left*) *Brick sill detail. (Photographer: Martin Charles. Courtesy of Building Design Partnership)*

(*Bottom left*) *Service yard. (Photographer: Martin Charles. Courtesy of Building Design Partnership)*

(*Top right*) *Exterior view of window detail. (Photographer: John Mills Photography Ltd. Courtesy of Building Design Partnership)*

(*Bottom right*) *Entrance hall to the two main levels. (Photograph: Courtesy of Building Design Partnership)*

and planting sympathetic to the suburban setting. Development of the design included a meeting with surrounding residents in January 1976 to assess reactions to the proposals.

The walls are clad in red-brown brickwork, and the pitched roofs are slate to blend with the surrounding houses.

The highly sophisticated control room, with consoles and special environmental services, was designed and coordinated by Building Design Partnership as an internal twenty-four-hour environment. This is in contrast to the ancillary accommodation and social rooms which are designed to provide a natural, outward-looking environment.

The considerable richness of brick modeling becomes important on the north facade to the main road, which is predominantly solid, broken only by the huge projecting window from the staff lounge, itself richly detailed, and two escape doors. The brick tower

enclosing the flues is enriched with detailed modeling. Everywhere the utilitarian is transformed, with a little attention and skill, into an object of interest. Consistent with the many diagonals in both the vertical and horizontal planes, the brick specially selected for use in great quantities is a cant. These are used not only on sills and lintels but also as string courses and column supports. String courses of brick on edge with slight corbeling are also freely used. Unfortunately, despite all the care in brick detailing, brick parapet walls are efflorescing, but this is probably a transitory problem. The terraces and courtyard are brick-paved. The elaborate patterning of diagonals and rectangles, and changes of level both of step height and of seat height, almost falls into the category of brick sculpture. Great use is made of projecting red stove-enameled aluminum drips and lapping cavity trays. These also give a horizontal emphasis to the brickwork.

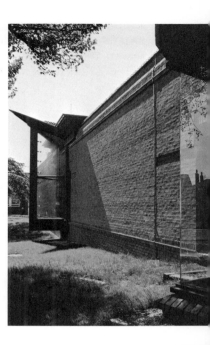

BAILEY RESIDENCE, KENSINGTON PLACE
London, England
ARCHITECT: Tom Kay Associates

ARCHITECT'S COMMENTS: The use of dense engineering bricks caused some damp penetration problems. The dense bricks are themselves waterproof and therefore incapable of absorbing water during periods of heavy or prolonged rain. Due to this fact, the mortar joints are exceptionally heavily loaded with water, because there is a near 100 percent run-off from the bricks themselves. The joints are quickly saturated and the water soon runs free down the internal surface of the outer leaf of the wall within the cavity. Theoretically, the cavity is a barrier, provided that there are no building imperfections, such as bridging of the cavity by mortar or mortar droppings on the wall ties. In this case, small areas of the wall were opened up, the cavity cleaned and rebuilt.

The staircase was built using an inner skin of standard bricks and an outer skin of "standard special" bricks, namely "double cant" bricks. In this way it was possible to produce the internal radius of 3 feet and the outer radius of 3 feet 11 inches, while maintaining the use of the stretcher bond.

Wall-mounted light fittings and shelf brackets are precast concrete, designed to fit the brick module.

Exterior view. (Photographer: Christopher Bailey)

(Top) Interior stair with polyethylene water pipe used as handrail. (Photographer: Christopher Bailey)

(Bottom) Interior view showing study/spare bedroom on gallery. (Photographer: Christopher Bailey)

KEBLE COLLEGE
**Oxford,
England / 1980**

**ARCHITECT: Ahrends
Burton & Koralek,
Architects**

ARCHITECT'S COMMENTS: These residential
rooms for Keble College, Oxford, were
designed to be constructed in two phases on
an extremely constricted site, with the
implicit understanding that the new building
would coexist sympathetically with the
extraordinary High Church–Anglican–Gothic
inventions of William Butterfield, built a
century ago. Phase 3 consisted of various
alterations to the existing buildings.

   The new building was conceived as a
"wall," one room thick, each room having a
two-way aspect for both view and ventilation,
the wall coiling around the southern end of
the site to enclose a new quadrangle. An
austere exterior perimeter of brick,
punctuated by vertical service towers and
slot windows, emphasizes the "wall" idea,
while on the inside of its protective shell
is a soft underbelly of glass formed of
overlapping planes which descend to shelter
a continuous walkway.

(*Below*) *Residential building, exterior view.*
(*Photographer: John Donat Photography*)

(*Above*) *Residential building, exterior view.* (*Photographer: John Donat
Photography*)

LEISURE TIME CENTRE, CONGREGATIONAL CENTRE
Hervanta, Tampere, Finland / 1979
ARCHITECT: Raili & Reima Pietila

ARCHITECT'S COMMENTS*:   The new town of Hervanta was planned by Professor Ruusauvuori. The complex of civic buildings in the central axis was to be in the spirit of (the region) Tampere. Thus the architecture . . . had to contain reminiscences of the Tammerkoski Falls area, and the predominant building material had to be red brick. This red brick was used in many forms to give each axis building an identity different from its neighbors. Another idea was that each group of buildings should embody an architecture of its own. As construction is due to go on into the 1990s, Finnish architecture will be taking new directions and we are allowing this natural development to mirror itself in each new building.

The Leisure Time Center and Congregational Center hint at a rather historical architecture. The tower of the former resembles the bastion of a castle and

the wall encircling this pair of buildings a city wall, with the exception that its windows open outward from the city toward the Park (lakefront). From inside, the windows seem to channel one's eyes down toward the water, and up toward the trees and sky.

From the outside, the semicolumns and gaps between the walls give the impression of a spruce's trunk and the mass of its branches. . . . The appearance . . . has taken on a certain local rustic quality from the use of wood with green surfaces, the dominant white skylights, and the wall of red brick.

In the Congregational Center the importance was to relate the color scale to nature. . . . The shopping center differs in that it resembles a turn-of-the-century (Finnish) railway station. Moreover, its elevations recall the vaulted windows of the Tampere Market Hall. This "inside hall" type of building (with) a big, warm interior and winter garden possesses leisurely, dawdling characteristics, is casual and entertaining . . . serves commercial purposes . . . makes a fitting civic building.

*Excerpted from the Finnish architectural review *Arkkitehti*, no. 5, June, 1979.

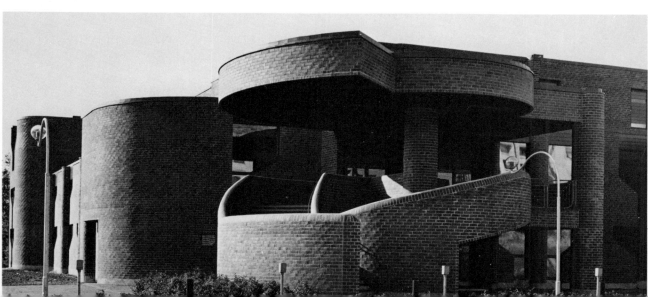

(Top) Exterior. (Photographer: Juhani Riekkolo)

(Bottom) Exterior view. (Photographer: Juhani Riekkolo)

(Upper) Exterior view. (Photographer: Juhani Riekkolo)

(Lower) Exterior view. (Photographer: Juhani Riekkolo)

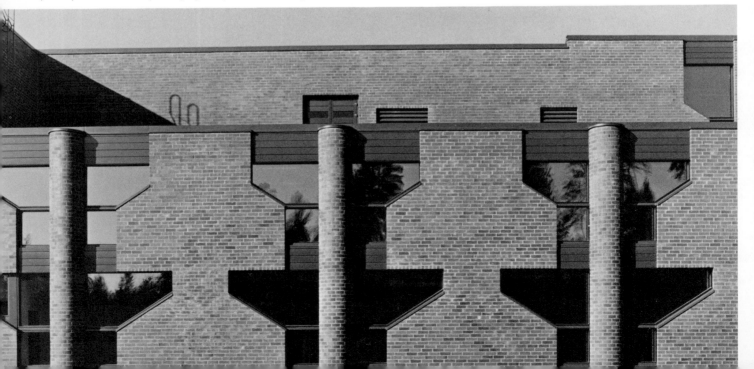

NEBENZAHL HOUSE
**Jerusalem,
Israel / 1972**

**ARCHITECT: Ahrends
Burton & Koralek**

ARCHITECT'S COMMENTS: The site in the Jewish quarter of the Old City of Jerusalem, just inside the Old City wall, overlooks the western wall, the Temple Mount, and Dome of the Rock with magnificent views ranging from Mount Zion and the Valley of Kidron, to the Mount of Olives and Mount Scopus, with the hills of the Judean Desert in the far distance.

The brief called for three separate apartments, each on a single level, with a common entrance court and a guest flat at ground level. Views from the building and its location played an extremely important part in the brief, not only for their scenic value but also because of their powerful religious and emotional content and associations. Legislation required that all external surfaces —including walls, roofs, and pavings—be of stone.

The house was designed to blend unobtrusively into the Old City without resorting to a pastiche of traditional buildings, but achieving a sense of quality with simplicity and without ostentation or pretension.

(Upper) Exterior view with garage at bottom right. Private home overlooking western wall, the Temple Mount, and Dome of the Rock, designed to blend into the Old City. (Photographer: Paul Koralek)

(Lower) Exterior view. Private home overlooking western wall, the Temple Mount, and Dome of the Rock, designed to blend into the Old City. (Photographer: Paul Koralek)

MUGHAL SHERATON HOTEL

Agra, India / 1976

ARCHITECT: **Arcop Design Group,**
Ramesh Khosla,
Ranjit Sabikhi, Ajoy Choudhury;
Anil Verma & Associates, Ray Affleck
LANDSCAPE ARCHITECT: **Ravindra Bhan**

The hotel, located near Taj Mahal, began operation in 1976. To express the spirit of traditional Mughal architecture in a contemporary medium, the project revived the local brick-making industry, used locally quarried marble, employed local manufacturers and artisans. It expresses the rich architectural tradition of the region.

(*Above*) *Exterior view—close-up of fountain and brickwork.* (*Photographer: Dinesh Sareen—The Aga Kahn Award for Architecture*)

(*Below*) *Exterior view showing central court with swimming pool.* (*Photographer: Copyright © Christopher Little—The Aga Kahn Award for Architecture*)

SAN GIUSEPPE PARISH CENTER
Monza, Italy / 1979
ARCHITECT: Dr. Justus Dahinden

ARCHITECT'S COMMENTS: The dynamics of this structure as we move from the outside inward is expressed in the shape of the spiral, that is, the shape that integrates concentration and expansion. The spiral is shown as an archetype in the hexagram of primordial symbols.

The dividing walls have grown as if by chance; this, then, is an architecture which nowhere imposes itself dogmatically or categorically. The volumes seek, in their texture, to be spontaneous and vital. Within the framework of the harmony-discord duality obtaining in architecture, the principle of discord prevails, which rests on disharmonic relationships and as such is the underlying form of life. Asymmetry is the dominant expression; in other words, there is no abstract organization or perceptible subjection to any kind of system. The use of brick lends itself well to the design concept.

(*Upper*) *Exterior view. (Photographer: Foto Studio Casali)*
(*Lower left*) *Exterior view. (Photographer: Foto Studio Casali)*
(*Lower right*) *Interior view. (Photographer: Foto Studio Casali)*

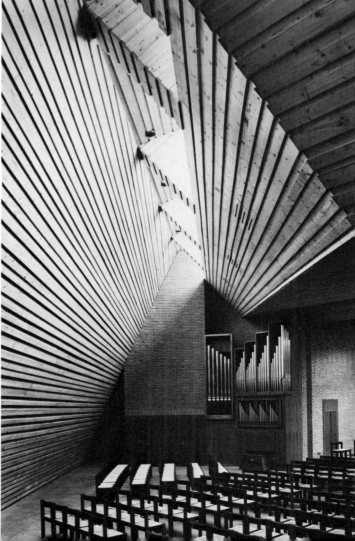

PRIVATE CLINIC PIO XI
Rome, Italy / 1970
ARCHITECT: Julio Lafuente

ARCHITECT'S COMMENTS: The Pio XI Clinic was constructed on an area on the Via Aurelia which was zoned for private dwellings. This zoning allows for a certain architectural liberty since it imposes only limits of height and boundaries.

This freedom of planning resulted in a totally articulated complex in which the patients' rooms, technical and sanitary facilities, and other areas are defined. This concept avoids the preestablished "boxing" of a given volume as happens in the more traditional-conservative ways of constructing these facilities.

The patients' rooms total 150 beds. The rooms are built following a "T" formation which provides an east-south orientation giving them isolation from street noises.

The medical and technical staff are situated in the northwest portion of the T and are in a central area with respect to the patients' rooms and are well serviced by elevators.

Radiology, surgery, and maternity are placed each one floor above the other. The nurses' quarters are on the last floor and the entrance is at street level.

To shorten the distances between departments, the building was designed in a compact manner but nevertheless with apertures and perforations that break the basic shell and allow as much natural light as possible to reach every part of it. This also discloses the planimetric distribution of each floor and allows the architectural design to be expressed on the exterior.

The structure is made of reinforced concrete with sand brick, the same material utilized in the interior of the chapel and in the entrance hall.

The chimneys, the air shafts, and the mechanical plant have been camouflaged so as to create an "architectural walk."

(Top opposite) View of entrance. (Photographer: Julio Lafuente)

(Bottom left) Floor plan—first floor.

(Bottom opposite) Exterior view showing mechanical air shafts. (Photographer: Julio Lafuente)

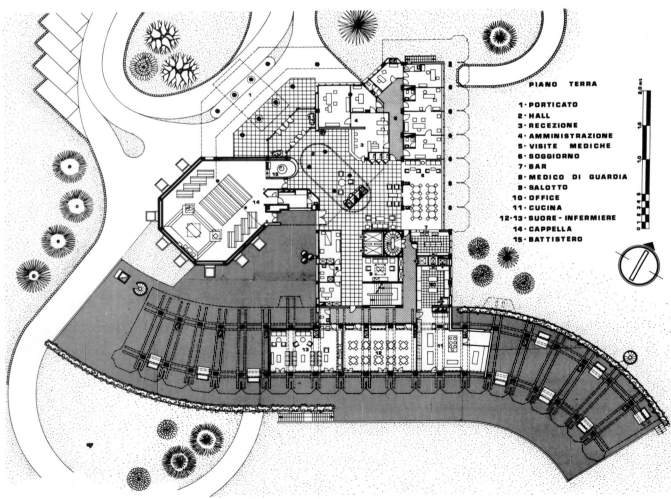

PIANO TERRA

1 · PORTICATO
2 · HALL
3 · RECEZIONE
4 · AMMINISTRAZIONE
5 · VISITE MEDICHE
6 · SOGGIORNO
7 · BAR
8 · MEDICO DI GUARDIA
9 · SALOTTO
10 · OFFICE
11 · CUCINA
12·13 · SUORE - INFERMIERE
14 · CAPPELLA
15 · BATTISTERO

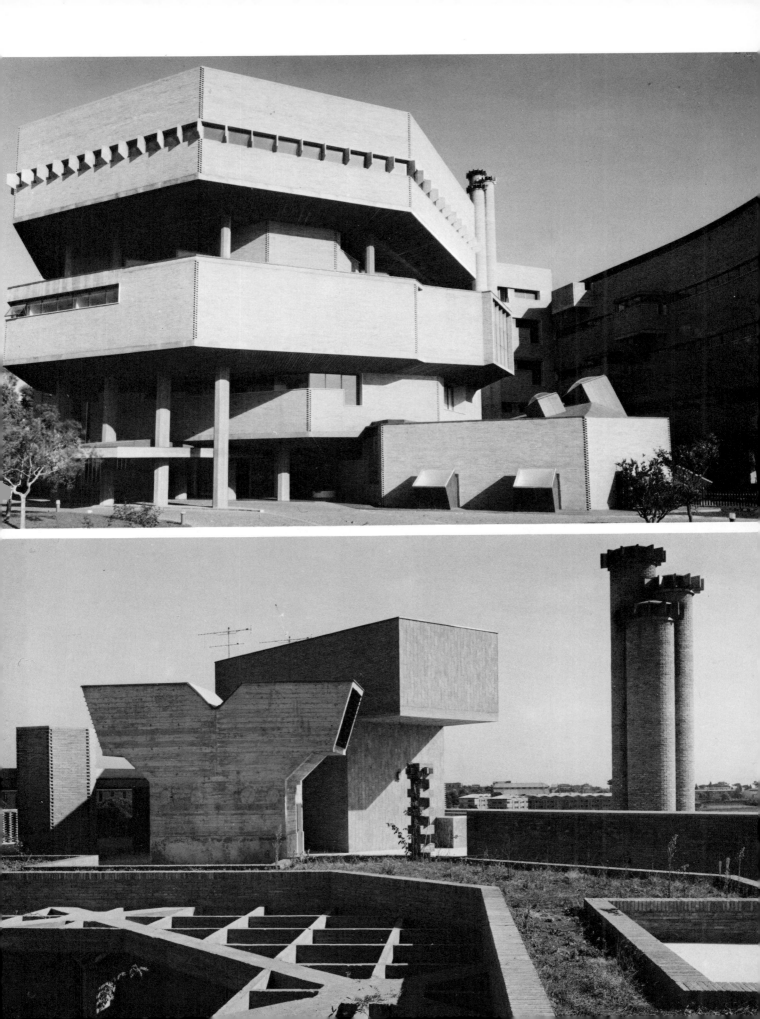

(*Top*) Ventilation stacks. (Photographer: Julio Lafuente)

(*Bottom*) Interior view of chapel. (Photographer: Julio Lafuente)

SANCTUARY OF COLLEVALENZA
Todi, Italy / 1968
ARCHITECT: Julio Lafuente

(Top) *View of bell tower. (Photographer: Julio Lafuente)*

(Bottom) *Close-up of brickwork. (Photographer: Julio Lafuente)*

(Top) View of interior stairway.
(Photographer: Julio Lafuente)

(Bottom) Interior. (Photographer: T. Okamura)

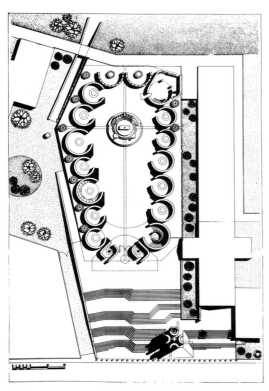

(Top) Site plan.

(Bottom) View of facade. (Photographer:
T. Okamura)

AGRICULTURAL CENTER
Nianing, Senegal / 1977
ARCHITECTS: UNESCO Architects

A prototype building system developed by
UNESCO architectural experts, based on a
concept of short-span barrel vaults, was
recognized for excellence by the Aga Khan
Award for Architecture. The building
concept, emphasizing the use of simple
construction techniques and easily accessible
local materials (concrete block), was used to
build an agricultural training school in
Nianing, Senegal.

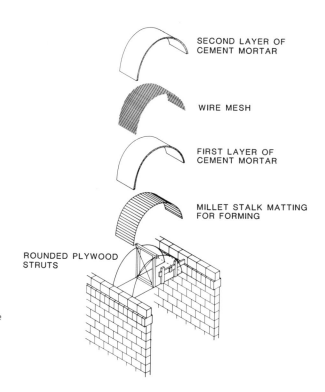

SECOND LAYER OF
CEMENT MORTAR

WIRE MESH

FIRST LAYER OF
CEMENT MORTAR

MILLET STALK MATTING
FOR FORMING

ROUNDED PLYWOOD
STRUTS

*(Top) Building system for short-span barrel vault.
(Photographer: Copyright © Christopher Little — The
Aga Khan Award for Architecture)*

*(Bottom) Exterior view. (Photographer: Copyright ©
Christopher Little — The Aga Khan Award for
Architecture)*

Interior view. (Photographer: Copyright © Christopher Little—The Aga Khan Award for Architecture)

SINGLE FAMILY HOME
Montras, Costa Brava, Spain / 1974

**ARCHITECT: Ricardo Bofill—
Taller de Arquitectura**

(Upper) View of pool area. (Photographer: Serena Vergano)

(Lower) Photographer: Serena Vergano

THE PYRAMID (HOMAGE TO CATALUNYA)
Marca Hispanica Park, le Perthus, Spain,
at the French-Spanish border / 1977

ARCHITECT: Ricardo Bofill—Taller de Arquitectura

ARCHITECT'S COMMENTS: The underlying purpose for this monument was the creation of a national symbol, that is, a structure which would express the identity of Catalonia in space and time. The chosen location is appropriate, having a central position in the ancient Marca Hispanica, which is today divided between Spain and France. During the development of the project, the pyramid form emerged.

Using local material of stone and red and yellow brick, the artist created an imposing approach to the top of the pyramid by the steep 2-foot-high brick risers. The ascent is bordered with stylized brick plant forms. The climax at the top is in the form of four turned columns of different sizes and shapes also made of brick.

The four pillars symbolize the mutilated fingers of the medieval hero Wifredo el Velloso who, before dying, pulled them across his shield, saying "Here is your banner!" And the flag of Catalonia in fact shows four red stripes on a golden ground.

(*Upper*) *General view.* (Photographer: Serena Vergano)

(*Lower*) *Close-up of detail.* (Photographer: Serena Vergano)

MITYANA MARTYR'S SHRINE
**Mityana, Uganda, South Africa /
1968**

ARCHITECT: Justus Dahinden

ARCHITECT'S COMMENTS: The church and parish center of Mityana commemorated in 1968 the canonization of the first African martyrs. The church is the focal point of a larger integrated complex of social and ecclesiastical buildings comprised of school, hospital, social center, Carmelite convent, vicarage, parish hall, and nursery.

The primary intention for the design was to adapt the architecture to the climatic conditions and the local culture and in particular the symbolic consciousness. In this respect the symbolic aspect of this church is both direct and obtuse. The three "cone segments" express particular spatial qualities: baptistery with men's choir, separate areas for nuns, with a tabernacle and confessionals. These segments are at the same time an ancient Bantu building symbol of which the liturgical dimension is very marked. In addition they also imitate authentic African dwellings, and one could say they are a biotectonic reflection of similar forms found in the vegetation of the country. As to the representation of the three honored martyrs, the three cone segment facings are arranged around a central place as a very clear symbolism.

The site and vegetation played an important role in the choice of forms and materials. The hot climate and humidity, added to the intense equatorial sun, led the buildings to be oriented east-west and equipped with wide eaves. Further local building materials such as bricks for the walls and floors, and wood for the ceilings were used. The segments of the cone are prefabricated reinforced concrete which was later sprayed with a waterproofing concrete dyed red, and this unity of color, between the red cones and red earth, further enforces the intention of adapting the architecture to the site.

The church as a meeting place for the community is an open house integrating interior courts and an atrium partially covered with tenting, situated so that access to the service can be gained from all sides. Processional spaces and a triumphal entrance were avoided, and the only formal element addressing entry is a drum platform linking the inner and outer spaces of the church.

*General view.
(Photograph: Courtesy
of Justus Dahinden)*

(Top) The drum platform. (Photograph: Courtesy of Justus Dahinden)

(Bottom) Interior view of chapel. (Photograph: Courtesy of Justus Dahinden)

CHAPTER FOUR

Masonry as an Art Form

The general interest in public art during the past several decades has stimulated architect and artist to rediscover new art possibilities for masonry.

As was pointed out in the first chapter, the use of brick as a material for art expression in the form of sculptural bas-reliefs goes as far back in history as the Babylonian period, 575–530 B.C. In modern times, the ancient technique of using premolded shapes from unbaked clay was used by Henry Moore in his famous brick mural for the Rotterdam Bouwcentrum building in 1955. In some respects this set a precedent, the influence of which is just now being felt. Presently the use of brick as an art form, integrated with the structure, is being used successfully in the United States and in many countries. In addition to the premolded technique, bas-reliefs made of standard masonry units give the architect and the artist an opportunity to create art forms. Colored, enameled glazed bricks add another dimension in the designs for interior as well as exterior wall areas. Modern diamond saws facilitate the cutting of the bricks to any desired size or shape.

A factor to consider is the relatively inexpensive way to introduce the human touch of the artist into the building design. Of utmost importance is to include this special brick art form in the preliminary design stages and in the construction budget.

I believe that this important trend, as illustrated in this chapter, will continue to accelerate and add human interest, excitement, and delight to the total environment.

SCHOOL DISTRICT #60 ADMINISTRATION BUILDING
Pueblo, Colorado

ARCHITECT: **Hurtig, Gardner, Froelich**
ARTIST: **Ken Williams**

ARCHITECT'S COMMENTS: A key element of the design is the semioval board room section that juts out from the main body of the building, which is essentially triangular in shape. Adding special interest is the brick bas-relief that runs almost the entire course of the curving 167-foot-long, 9-foot-high exterior wall of the board room segment.

Created by Ken Williams, an artist who has crafted brick sculptures for other buildings in the Pueblo area, this work hints at southwest themes but is basically abstract. It uses space and line to express the sculptural possibilities of brick, just as the structure as a whole does.

Brick was chosen because it lends itself to the regional architecture, suggesting a linkage to the old adobe buildings of the southwest. Other reasons: brick's durability and easy maintenance, plus its feeling of warmth and quality. The brick walls are load-bearing,

Exterior view showing brick bas-relief 167 feet long, 9 feet high. (Photograph: Courtesy of Hurtig, Gardner, Froelich)

providing a total structural support system.

Standard size off-white brick was used, with some units cut to 45-degree and 60-degree angles as needed for such uses as the top of parapet walls, light standards, building corners, and window sills.

The overall design concept of the District 60 Administration Building had the pragmatic goal of developing the most square footage, in addition to parking areas, out of the one square block available for the project. The result: 42,000 square feet of space on three levels—a finished basement and two stories. But in order to avoid a static building line following street patterns, the architects cut the square along a diagonal to form a basically triangular structure that fronts on the street at an angle looking toward downtown Pueblo.

Exterior view. (Photograph: Courtesy of Hurtig, Gardner, Froelich)

OFFICE OF LOUIS G. REDSTONE ASSOCIATES, INC.

Livonia, Michigan / 1976

ARCHITECT: **Louis G. Redstone Associates, Inc.**
MURAL DESIGN: **Louis G. Redstone, FAIA**

ARCHITECT'S COMMENTS: In my forty-five years of architectural practice, the integration of art as part of the building structure has been the "trademark" of my office. It was only natural that from the conceptual design stage, a mural was included as part of the building structure.

In this mural, as in others, I like to use colorful ceramic inserts, created by professional ceramists, for added "spark" and interest. The working drawings for the mural show the projected and indented brick-detailed dimensions.

(Upper) Exterior view at entrance. (Photographer: Balthazar Korab)

(Lower) view of brick mural at entrance. (Photographer: Balthazar Korab)

w of brick mural from lobby. (Photographer: Balthazar Korab)

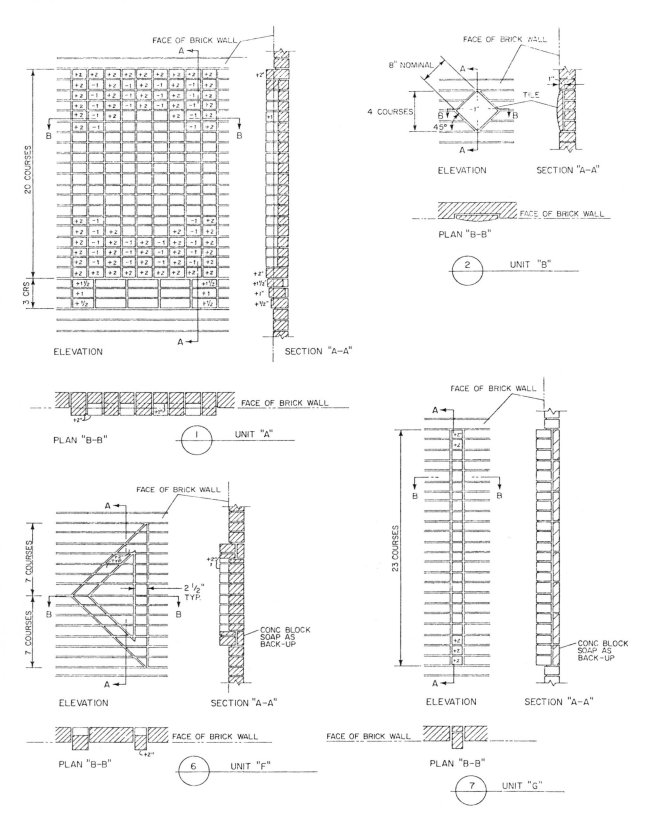

Working drawing for brick mural.

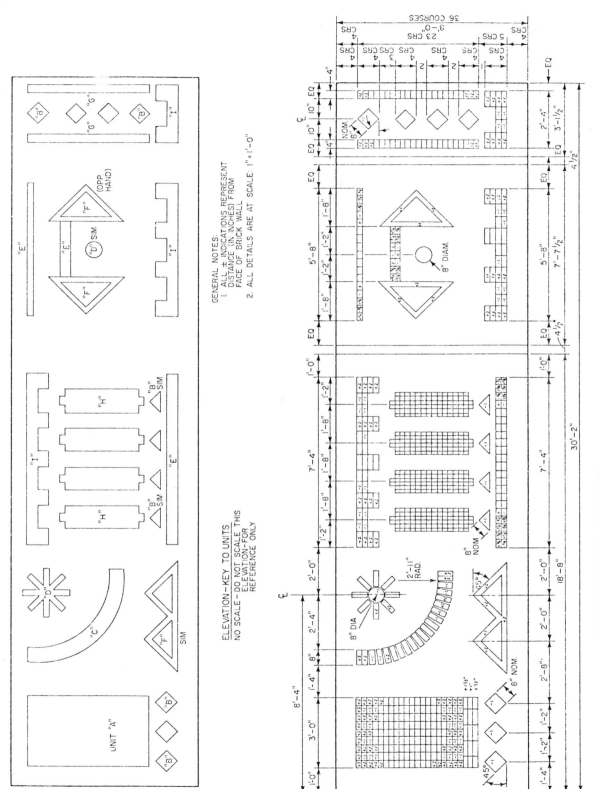

ELEVATION – KEY TO UNITS
NO SCALE – DO NOT SCALE THIS
ELEVATION – FOR
REFERENCE ONLY

GENERAL NOTES:
1. ALL ± INDICATIONS REPRESENT DISTANCE (IN INCHES) FROM FACE OF BRICK WALL
2. ALL DETAILS ARE AT SCALE: 1" = 1'-0"

ELEVATION – MURAL WALL AT ENTRANCE
SCALE: 1/2" = 1'-0"

Elevation mural wall at entrance and elevation key to units.

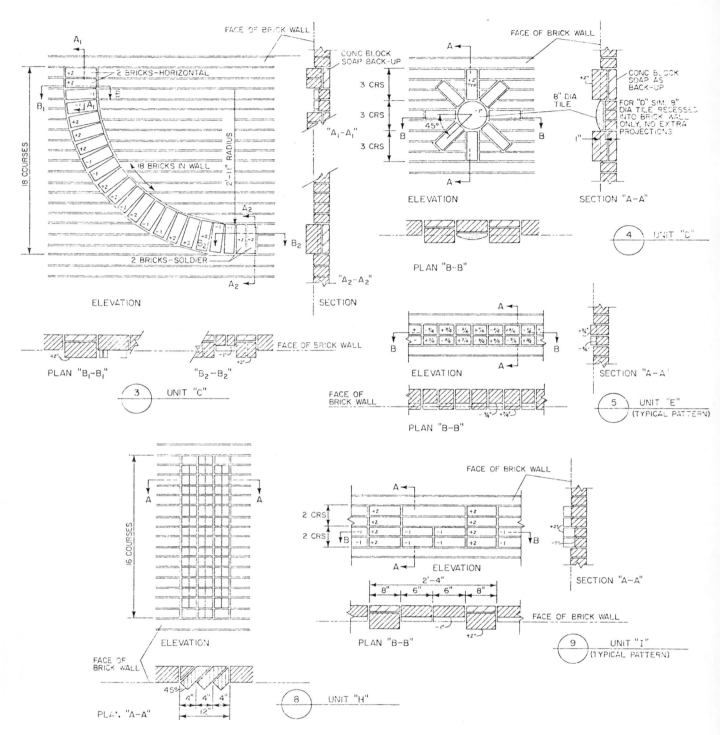

Typical patterns.

FIRST FEDERAL OF MICHIGAN, OPERATION CENTER

Troy, Michigan / 1973

ARCHITECT: **Louis G. Redstone Associates, Inc.**
MURAL DESIGN: **Louis G. Redstone, FAIA**

ARCHITECT'S COMMENTS: The location of the operations center at a busy intersection, plus functional program requirements and a need for energy efficiency, resulted in a design in which exterior walls are essentially windowless. However, an interior court was provided, within view of most spaces on both floors and accessible from the employees' cafeteria. A 40 foot by 60 foot brick and ceramic mural in the court, combined with attractive landscaping, plus the generous use of color and fabrics in the office decor provides eye relief and generates interest in the environment.

(Top) Interior view of lounge looking out onto court. (Photographer: Balthazar Korab)

(Bottom) View of court. (Photographer: Balthazar Korab)

JEWISH COMMUNITY CENTER
West Bloomfield Township,
Michigan / 1975

ARCHITECT: Louis G. Redstone
Associates, Inc.
MURAL DESIGN: Louis G. Redstone, FAIA

ARCHITECT'S COMMENTS: The mural *Eternal Hope* expresses two symbolic ideas of Jewish life. On the right side the broken menorah symbolizes the Holocaust; on the left side the two growing stems reaching upward symbolize the eternal striving for Jewish survival. The design of the lower portion is derived from segments found in the floor design of an ancient synagogue in Israel.

The design unifies all the elements of the mural to become an integral part of the architecture. Standard brick units were used.

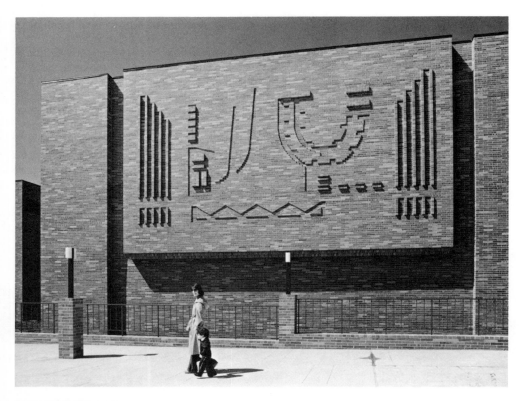

Close-up view of brick mural. (Photograph: Courtesy of Louis G. Redstone)

View of brick mural. (Photographer: Balthazar Korab)

COUNCIL HOUSE EAST
**Union Housing for the
Elderly, St. Louis,
Missouri / 1970**

**ARCHITECT: Schwarz & Henmi
SCULPTORS: Wiliam C.
Severson &
Saunders Schultz—SCOPIA**

SCULPTORS' COMMENTS: The 250-foot-high
bas-relief required the skills of three trades:
the bricklayers, the tuck-pointers, and the
pointers. The masons laid the recessed areas
according to diagrams drawn on the
underlying concrete by the artists who were
on the job daily, working about a story and a
story and a half above the heads of the
bricklayers.

The tuck-pointers later cut the corners off
bricks to create the smooth contours and also
ground deeper recessions in some of the
sweeping curves for a stronger visual effect.
The painters put a stain sealer on the recessed
areas to make the design "read" from 2 miles
away.

Photographer: Rudy Schultz

DR. B. BENEDICT GLAZER ELEMENTARY SCHOOL
Detroit, Michigan / 1968

ARCHITECT: Louis G. Redstone Associates, Inc.
ARTIST: Narendra Patel

Inner court – glazed brick mural 24 feet by 12 feet. (Photographer: Daniel Bartush)

Covered walkway. Glazed brick mural The Four Seasons *– 100 feet long. (Photograph: Courtesy of Louis G. Redstone)*

LOEW'S ANATOLE HOTEL
Dallas, Texas / 1979
ARCHITECT: Beran & Shelmire
DEVELOPER: Trammel Crow
ARTIST: Mara Smith

ARCHITECT'S COMMENTS: A recent example of teamwork of the developer, architect, artist, and mason contractor is demonstrated in the Anatole Hotel in Dallas, Texas. Brick was the choice of the developer and architect. To ensure the right color, texture, pattern, and other details relating to brick involved research in a number of cities, including Washington, D.C., and Williamsburg, Virginia, to explore the varieties of brick used in completed structures, old and new. The painstaking course of selection—a process of elimination—included a review of various mock-ups of different brick types and colors.

The chosen brick from Endicott Clay Products, Endicott, Nebraska, is an iron-spot brick made from clay bearing traces of natural iron ore. According to the mason contractor, the brick for the Anatole seems to change hue, depending on the angle of the light. Sometimes it has a rosy cast, resulting from the basic red clay body, while at other times it takes on a bluish cast from the clay-iron compound formed during flashing. As for size, a larger than standard unit was chosen—$3\frac{5}{8}$ inches by $3\frac{5}{8}$ inches by $11\frac{5}{8}$ inches. The developer and the architect felt the larger size brick would be better related proportionally to the mass of the building.

Brick mural. (Photograph: Courtesy of Loew's Anatole Hotel)

The initial design concept included five large panels approximately 15 feet by 18 feet and 15 feet by 22 feet. Mara Smith was chosen from a limited competition of five artists. From preliminary sketches to the final installation of the panels, the process took eighteen months of concentrated work. Once the subject was approved, the artist transferred the design to the wet clay by carving and shaping to fit the established brick courses. Using a curved knife, a saw blade, and a drill, Ms. Smith carved the details up to a depth of $2\frac{1}{2}$ inches. After finishing a panel, each brick had to be turned over to be numbered and then stacked on a large pallet. After being loaded onto the pallets, the bricks were left to dry for a month, then put into a kiln for a week and fired. Finally after a month of cooling, they were loaded onto a train and shipped to Dallas.

Ms. Smith did most of the brick unloading herself and reconstructed the murals on the ground at the Anatole, following the row and position number she had written on each brick.

From that point, the masons had the exciting experience of installing the murals and becoming a part of the art process.

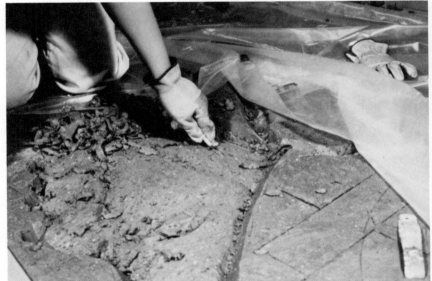

(Top) Cutting detail using saw blade. (Photograph: Courtesy of Mara Smith; Photographer: E. R. Hall)

(Middle) Incising detail in clay. (Photograph: Courtesy of Mara Smith; Photographer: E. R. Hall)

(Bottom) Mason installing mural panel. (Photograph: Courtesy of Mara Smith. Photographer: E. R. Hall)

VETERINARY MEDICAL TEACHING HOSPITAL
Oregon State University
Corvallis, Oregon

ARCHITECT: Payne Settecase Smith Doss, Architecture
ARTIST: Jacques Overhoff

The design approach was to create a tapestry
effect from brick components to be
installed according to the standard methods
of brick masonry construction.

*Exterior view showing brick bas-relief mural, 16 feet
by 36 feet.*

REGENCY SQUARE LIBRARY
Jacksonville, Florida / 1976
ARCHITECT: Pappas Associates Architects, Inc.

ARCHITECT'S COMMENTS: The "skintle" brick wall serves as a focal point of the interior circulation area. This wall is constructed of bricks projecting at differing degrees with random voids to excite the pattern. It was designed by our office and is a heavy patterned pierced wall. It is on axis with the entry doors and acts as a visual terminus while, at the same time, screening off access to the toilet rooms behind. Specifically, a skintled wall is a sculptured brick wall with varying degrees of protrusions and voids in combination with headers, stretchers, rowlocks, and soldier courses.

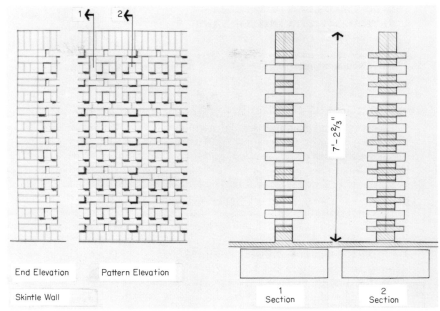

(Top) Skintle wall elevations and sections. (Photograph: Courtesy of Pappas Associates Architects, Inc.)

(Bottom) Interior brick wall. (Photograph: Courtesy of Pappas Associates Architects, Inc.)

NATIONAL WESTMINISTER BANK
Stoke-on-Trent, England / 1976

ARCHITECT: Wood, Goldstraw & Yorath
ARTIST: Walter Ritchie

SCULPTOR'S COMMENTS: From many "idea sketches" I make a small-scale drawing to show my client. If this is approved I next make a full-size drawing in charcoal. The latter drawing is not "squared up" from the smaller one. Enlargement demands redrawing to take into account different angles of vision and different proportions. This second drawing is usually much livelier than the first one.

From the charcoal drawing I again sketch freely onto the stone, brick, or other material, but this time I may take a few measurements. At all stages of drawing and carving I use a mirror, which reduces a work so that all its parts may be seen in relation. The reverse image also corrects any astigmatism of the eye and gives new and often surprising aspects of the work in hand.

For the first stage of carving stone or brick, I might use a 3- or 4-pound hammer with a "pitcher," a broad, thick type of chisel which, with a quick heavy blow, shocks off large pieces of material. The pitcher is followed by a "punch" used at 45 degrees, and the rough forms are further developed by a "point" used with even, controlled blows at right angles to the emerging forms. The forms are further refined by a 1-inch "claw chisel." Punch, point, and claw all produce characteristic textures that may be left to make their contribution to the finished work.

Definition and delicate detail are obtained with a $\frac{1}{2}$-inch or smaller tungsten-tipped flat chisel. With patience, an extremely fine surface can be produced with this tool used with a 2-pound hammer—never a wooden mallet. Further smoothing to increase textural contrast is done with abrasives—Carborundum and silicon carbide, for example.

The brick panels are carved at my studio and moved to site. I prefer carving because this allows me complete control. The drawback to carving is the large amount of fine dust.

To facilitate transport, panels are laid with weak mortar joints at course levels that make suitable divisions with regard to structure and weight. When the carving is completed, these joints are sawed out with a tungsten-tipped masonry saw and wood slips inserted. Terylene straps, which will carry up to 3 tons and measure less than the thickness of a joint, can then be used to lift the section away.

Brick sculpture Hanley Girl, *9 feet 5 inches high. (Photographer: S. L. Taylor)*

Brick sculpture Hanley Girl, 9 feet 5 inches high. (Photographer: Walter Ritchie)

PRIMARY SCHOOL
at the Medical
Faculties,
Woluwe-St-Lambert,
Brussels, Belgium /
1975

ARCHITECT: L. Kroll

ARCHITECT'S COMMENTS: The outside of the
school was a field of creativity for the
bricklayers. We told them that we wanted
varied materials such as different bricks and
stones of different forms for the recreation
area of the children. We proposed the general
shape and dimension, and they did it
following their own ideas.

ARCHITECT'S COMMENTS: The sculpture
figures were done by ordinary bricklayers.
We proposed little models (without scale) and
they did it by themselves; we did not draw
the details, the workers invented them. We
asked the Ministry of Culture to give them an
award, but the ministry classified the
sculptures as "popular art." We didn't want
that segregation.

(Top) Brick figures. (Photograph: Courtesy of L. Kroll)
(Bottom) Brick sculpture. (Photograph: Courtesy of L. Kroll)

GROUNDS NEAR PROVINCIALE WATERSTAAD
Middleburg, Holland / 1975

ARTIST: Sander Littel
ARCHITECT: Berghoef, Hondius & Lamers

Environmental sculpture, 30 feet by 111 feet, red granite rocks. (Photographer: Stichting "Kunst en Bedrijf")

FIRE STATION
Hedera, Israel

Brick mural. (Photographer: Louis G. Redstone)

PLACE DES GEANTS
Villeneuve, Grenoble, France / 1980

SCULPTOR: **Klaus Schultze**

SCULPTOR'S COMMENTS: The sculptor likes to tell fairytale stories with his art. Here is depicted the story of two giants, a man and woman, awakening in the morning, climbing up the stairs, crossing the plaza, curious to explore our world. At the end they disappear into the ground.

Usually the sculptures have a concrete core, as in the case of *Rue Mademoiselle* in Paris and *La Facade* in Zurich.

Because of weight problems in Grenoble, the figures are formed by a framework of wire netting and concrete and then covered with bricks.

I never use any special bricks. The bricks are made in a small, old factory near Paris, named Vaugirard. The quality is that of a handmade appearance in form and color. The bricks are cut and shaped in my studio. There the glazing is also done.

These fantasy figures give children and adults alike much enjoyment. They excite the imagination as new elements are discovered by the passerby.

(Top) View of plaza showing brick sculpture. (Photograph: Courtesy of Klaus Schultze)

(Bottom) Glazed brick sculpture. (Photograph: Courtesy of Klaus Schultze)

Facade. (Photograph: Courtesy of Klaus Schultze)

SCULPTURED WALL
Rue Mademoiselle,
Paris, France / 1977

SCULPTOR: Klaus Schultze

Wall 300 feet long, around a school. Brick over concrete forms. Standard size bricks are cut and shaped. Glazing is done by sculptor in his studio. (Photograph: Courtesy of Klaus Schultze)

TOWNE CENTER
Rodez,
France / 1976

TOWN PLANNER:
M. Coupat
ARTIST: Klaus
Schultze

(Top) Fountain configuration with brickwork. (Photograph: Courtesy of Klaus Schultz)

(Bottom) Fountain configuration with brickwork. (Photograph: Courtesy of Klaus Schultze)

Reclined Man, *18 feet high by 28 feet long, colored
and standard brick, placed on the front lawn of
complex. (Photographer: Jacques Verrier; Photograph: Courtesy of Klaus Schultze)*

LYCEE DE ST. CHERON
Essonne, France

SCULPTOR: Francis Burette

AUTHOR'S COMMENTS: In the French new cities, the planning for the outdoor public spaces of schools, libraries, and theaters, the architect and artist work together to create a natural and exciting environment. Brick is successfully used as a flexible material to produce the varied sculptural forms.

Brick sculptured fountain Fountaine. *(Photograph: Courtesy of Francis Burette)*

Brick sculpture Le Theatre. (Photograph: Courtesy of Francis Burette)

SCHOOL ENTRANCE COURT
New City of Cergy-Pontoise, France / 1977

ARCHITECT: Maneval
ARTISTS: Bernard Alleaume & Yvette Vincent-Alleaume

Photographer: Jacques Verrier; Photograph: Courtesy of Maneval

SAINT BERNADETTE CHURCH
Grand Quevilly, new Rouen, France

ARCHITECT: Henry Caron
ARTIST: Pierre Szekely

(Top) Close-up of nave. Brick and concrete relief Supernatural Intervention. *(Photographer: Pierre Joly et Vera Cardot)*

(Bottom) Interior of nave. Brick and concrete relief Supernatural Intervention. *(Photographer: Pierre Joly et Vera Cardot)*

GARDEN, ANDRE BLOC RESIDENCE
Meudon, France / 1966

ARCHITECT: **Andre Bloc**

Brick and concrete structure, 39 feet by 18 feet, Habitat #II. (Photographer: Gilles Ehrmann)

KANKAANPAA TOWN HALL
Kankaanpaa, Finland / 1967
ARCHITECT: **Kaija & Heikki Siren**
ARTIST: **Kauko Raike**

The three negative molds of this work were
formed of kips in the studio. They were then
taken to a brick factory where the unbaked
bricks were pushed against them to form the
required shapes, prior to putting them in the
kiln.

Brick relief. (Photographer: Pietinen; Photograph: Courtesy of the Museum of Finnish Architecture)

HAKAVOURI CHURCH
Helsinki, Finland / 1970
ARCHITECT: Eevi Aho
ARTIST: Pekka Kontio

(Top) Brick relief An Empty Tomb – close-up view. (Photographer: Esa Santakari; Photograph: Courtesy of The Museum of Finnish Architecture)

(Bottom) Brick relief An Empty Tomb. (Photographer: Esa Santakari; Photograph: Courtesy of the Museum of Finnish Architecture)

PROTESTANT CHURCH "CROSSROADS"
The Hague, Holland / 1969
ARCHITECT: K. J. van Nieukerken
ARTIST: Joop Beljon

ARCHITECT'S COMMENTS: In designing this church building, which represents a rigorous departure from the existing Protestant church building tradition, the artists have been given a central position. The realization of a spatial field of forces reflecting the human relation with the universe calls for a spiritual naiveté of the artist and increased attention for what is expressed and made perceptible by human emotions.

Only the artist is capable of disentangling him- or herself from an established sense of order and of giving expression to the complex of things temporal and universal which, because of their controversial nature, cannot be grasped in a functional pattern of thought.

The artist designs from an emotional activity which gropes for the motives governing life. This enables the creation of human surroundings which lack the constraints of reality.

My request to my friend Beljon was therefore of indispensable significance in order to be able to give expression to what the name of this building would in reality imply.

A case in point is that the restrained ruffle of the brick walls in which the bricks have been joined into a shape by hand, accentuates the visible tension in the building's space when only an acoustic adjustment was necessary.

This experiment demonstrates that the artist's visible touch intensifies the relation between a human being and the built environment. This provides a valuable addition to the current purely scientific approach to the building process.

(Below) Exterior view. (Photographer: Mike Toner)

(Opposite, top) Close-up of brick relief. (Photographer: Mike Toner)

(Opposite, bottom) Interior view showing brick relief. (Photographer: Mike Toner)

UNIVERSITY OF NYMEGEN, CAMPUS
Nymegen, Holland / 1974

ARCHITECT: Kraayvanger Associates
ARTIST: J. J. Beljon

Plaza, brick elements. (Photographer: Rob Meijer)

Fountain and plaza. (Photographer: Rob Meijer)

REFAJA HOSPITAL

Landscape, Dordrecht, Holland / 1977

ARCHITECTS:
Eykelenboom, Gerritse
& Middelhoek
ARTIST: Hans Petri
SCULPTURE FUNDED BY:
Hospital—fountain
cones; cultural
board of the
government of
Dordrecht—
the hills, crossed by
road and footpath;
public works services of
the government
of Dordrecht—rest of
environmental layout,
the greenery,
pavement, bus stop

Fountain, concrete pillars, highest 36 feet. (Photograph: Courtesy of Hans Petri)

Artificial hills 15 feet high, crossed by a road and foot path. Sides are covered with bricks and stones. (Photograph: Courtesy of Hans Petri)

CHAPTER FIVE

Technical Aspects of Masonry Construction

Contributors to this chapter are

WILLIAM LEFKOFSKY, P.E., *Structural Engineer*

LEO G. SHEA, FAIA, *President, Louis G. Redstone Associates, Inc.*

DONALD J. SMITH, *Architect, CSI, Louis G. Redstone Associates, Inc.*

RALPH J. STEPHENSON, P.E., *Consulting Engineer*

Masonry materials are used in nearly every phase of construction and are available in a bewildering range of materials, colors, and textures. On any given project might be found masonry products made from concrete, clay, ceramic, glass, gypsum, or even artificially created materials, all assembled in horizontal and vertical systems to serve varying purposes throughout the entire facility.

Of the major building components—substructure, superstructure, exterior skin, interior rough work, interior finish work, and systems—masonry may be an integral part, from minor to major, in any one, some, or all six components. Because of this versatility, great care must be taken by the architect and engineer to ensure that planning and scheduling for installation of masonry elements are properly considered during design.

Usually five major steps are taken in the design and construction process once design work starts:

1. Preparation of construction documents
2. Award of contracts
3. Procurement
4. Installation
5. Maintenance of materials

The last of these, maintenance, is a postconstruction activity. However, since the responsibility of the designer and the contractor extends beyond turnover of the facility, they certainly must consider the postcompletion design and construction implications inherent in using a masonry system of any type.

A factor of increasing importance to proper planning for the use of masonry and other building materials is the movement during the past 10 to 20 years toward project management forms other than those considered traditional. The emergence of prearranged design and construction teams has proved that a building program can be successfully accomplished by organizational systems other than when full contract documents are prepared and then followed by hard cost contract proposal, award, and construction. The need for greater flexibility than in the past for awarding construction contracts has often combined with the high cost of financing to create a desire on the part of the owner to occupy facilities at the earliest possible date. This, along with the demonstrated success of constant construction feedback into the design process has made it imperative that the owner, architect, engineer, contractor, and subcontractor all recognize and seriously consider both old and new forms of managing building programs in planning proper use of masonry.

Strongly affected by this rearrangement of managerial responsibilities are the masonry trades. Contemporary conditions have made it important that the ultimate installation of the masonry system be carefully considered as the design process proceeds. Thus, the designer must now evaluate each masonry unit selection for its design desirability, its procurement condition, the ease and economy of its erection, and, of course, its ultimate maintenance cost in the completed project.

For example, in certain instances it might prove desirable to preselect and perhaps even preorder masonry units where there is a possibility that, at the time of construction, such units would not be available. An instance of this was seen several years ago when a severe (but predictable) winter gas shortage forced the shutdown of many brick kilns in the midwest from early November on through to the next spring. Since masonry units were to have been selected from one of these manufacturer's standard product lines, a preordering of those materials certainly would have been proper to consider during design.

Successful use of masonry demands competent planning and scheduling attention by all members of the owner, design, and construction team. Let's examine the major building components and consider some of the factors that affect planning and scheduling the use of masonry during installation of the component. The components normally encountered in constructing a new facility are

1. **Site work** That work installed outside the building line but within the property line or contract limits.

2. **Substructure** Footings, foundation walls, pilings, caissons, and other related structural units which transmit building loads to the subsoil.

3. **Superstructure** Structural elements which directly or indirectly transmit building loads to the substructure.

4. **Exterior skin** Building elements used to enclose the structure from weather.

5. **Interior rough work** Portions of the building which, when installed, can be totally or partially exposed to weather without damage.

6. Interior finishes Items which must be partially or totally protected from weather to avoid damage.

7. Systems Components which collectively make up a total operating unit and can generally be identified as a separate and distinct work project.

Substructure

Starting from the substructure and working through installation of the finish trades gives a clear picture of how the architect, engineer, and contractor can help provide optimum design and field performance when using masonry materials.

Frequently masonry foundation walls are used in lieu of cast-in-place concrete. On light, simple buildings it may even be desirable to design a foundation that can utilize either material. Availability of concrete accessories and equipment varies from contractor to contractor and area to area. Even seasonal conditions and market fluctuations may affect the choice. Therefore, if it is possible to provide masonry alternatives to concrete foundation walls, or vice versa, cost and time savings of considerable extent may sometimes be realized.

Following this course of design action involves careful correlation of the foundation design with the superstructure design, and a consideration of the potential desires of those who are to bid upon the actual construction of the unit. It is also important to be certain that if masonry is to be used for the substructure, the specifications provide for all-weather maintenance of the erection operation. Delays in installation of early substructure elements can be disastrous to the schedule of a project just getting under way during the bad weather seasons of the year.

A situation in which the use of masonry structural elements often produces a faulty perception of cost saving is found when thickened floor slabs on grade are used to carry structural masonry bearing walls. The problem is that certain conditions, such as a frozen subbase or late release and delivery of underground materials, may delay construction of floor slabs on grade but might not necessarily delay erection of important vertical masonry units. Thus, if a block bearing wall on a thickened slab is essential to continuing construction of a structural steel frame, but because of cold weather the slab supporting the masonry cannot be poured, then a serious problem results.

It is usually a good idea, especially with bearing walls, to encourage consideration of a discretionary alternate proposal to install separate masonry wall footings for these walls with the substructure. This alternative may be felt to be too expensive during periods of favorable weather. However, long experience indicates that more often than not, when inclement weather or other slab delay factors are encountered, a thickened slab design with no such alternative allowed for separate footings can cause work disruption and expensive delays until the matter is resolved. This most often occurs by ultimately permitting or paying for the construction of such separate footings.

Superstructure

A most important requirement in using masonry as a part of the structural load carrying frame above grade is to understand thoroughly the interfacing of masonry with other structural materials such as steel, aluminum, concrete, or wood. Whenever masonry is used in conjunction with these to provide support to either vertical or horizontal structural components, the erection sequence must be carefully thought out during design so as not to impose expensive and limited erection approaches upon field operations.

In general, mixtures of wall bearing and fully framed structural designs should be viewed with caution. Occasionally successful, economical, well-run projects do make use of such mixed systems, but only when the mix has been carefully thought through during the design period and the combination system is recognized and understood by those proposing to build the facility.

If there is any question about whether a framed unit should be supported by a similar framing material or whether it should be made masonry-bearing, it usually is best to frame it with the similar materials. This is particularly true as structural components become smaller and smaller. For instance, to design a small canopy structure of steel columns and beams, and then to support one portion of this canopy on isolated brick piers could result in an expensive construction sequence that could be avoided either by fully framing it in steel, or by making all vertical supports of masonry.

Whenever mixed structural components are used, there is always the danger that varying procurement times and conditions may force contractors to make return trips to erect bits and pieces of one or the other of the components. Clean division lines between structural erection trades should be an important consideration in the designer's mind when using masonry as a structural component.

Another factor that must be carefully evaluated if masonry is intended to take structural loads, is to ensure that the designer investigates forces from all directions, both vertically and laterally. Masonry, well used, is a good structural material in compression, but unless specially reinforced has very little value in resisting tension or shear. Lateral loads that impose bending moments and high shear stresses must be identified early so that the masonry component can be designed and specified properly.

For instance, if a masonry dividing pier, restrained at one end by the floor structure, is to be used in a feature elevator of a hotel, the lateral loads imposed by possible horizontal movements of the elevator in the guide rails should be investigated as part of the material selection. Lack of such investigation during design might force expensive reinforcement, revision, or in some cases replacement of the system during construction.

Engineered Masonry

In the past, structural design of masonry was based on empirical data gathered over the years. It was conservative and had little technical basis but rather was a practical approach based on past performance. In recent years a new approach, "engineered masonry," has been developed. It is based on established engineering principles and reflects extensive materials testing, including laboratory testing of materials as well as field quality control during construction.

Using engineered masonry, there are essentially two ways to construct a masonry wall bearing system, for instance, for an apartment building: one method is to load the exterior and corridor walls (assuming a central corridor), and the other is to load the cross or shear walls. Generally, when the structure is over six stories, the preference is to load the cross walls and let compressive forces caused by gravity loads help offset the tensile forces caused by horizontal loads, which in turn reduces the reinforcing steel requirement in the walls.

Design of such masonry walls must be in accordance with the prevailing building codes, which permit masonry units of various strength levels. For simplicity, it is recommended that only two different masonry block strengths be utilized, if more than one is necessary, so as to have only one type of masonry unit on the project at any given time during construction. For example, on one eighteen-story masonry wall bearing structure, higher strength masonry was used up to the twelfth floor and lower strength masonry was used above the twelfth floor. All of the masonry walls, both bearing and nonbearing, were constructed of units of the same strength at each floor in order to eliminate the possibility of the wrong strength masonry unit being used inadvertently. The slight additional cost of this procedure is insignificant compared to the potential repair or removal procedures required to correct a substitution error.

In apartment buildings, precast concrete balconies are often used, constructed either of hollow core units with a sloped topping or of solid concrete. Aside from the code requirements for the design of balconies, railings must be analyzed separately for structural adequacy and, in particular, for thermal movement. This is particularly true of precast concrete railings.

On the example above, the architectural design featured both protruding and recessed balconies, not placed at the same location at each floor for similar units. This led to some balconies being placed directly over living units and required a separate analysis of waterproofing, heat transfer, and thermal movement.

There also were bearing walls starting at various floor levels and extending upward through several levels to carry these balconies. These walls had to be designed as cantilevers, utilizing the same principles as reinforced concrete, by placing 4 inches of grout with re-bars sandwiched between two 4-inch wythes of masonry. All deflections were limited to L/600, which is more than adequate to prevent cracking.

On another ten-story masonry wall bearing structure, the cross walls were used as bearing walls and were 8-inch block, while the exterior walls, both bearing and nonbearing, were 8-inch brick. One of the first considerations was the floor-to-floor height of the building to maintain masonry coursing. The interior wall layout had a central corridor with steel lintels over the corridor to support the precast concrete floor units, and the building width (inside dimension) was a multiple of the precast concrete widths.

The exterior nonbearing walls passed by the floors and were attached with flexible anchors to accomplish necessary wall bracing. With these walls placed outside of the floors, when the precast frame moves due to inherent pretensioned forces, these walls are not disturbed. In addition, the natural camber in the floor does not have to be accommodated by the mason in constructing these walls, but the gap between the wall and the floor edge must be firestopped.

Some of the bearing walls had large openings at the ground level to accommodate community rooms, mechanical rooms, and so on. These openings are obviously limited by structural requirements, but the ground-to-second floor height can be increased to ease headroom restrictions.

In summary, the floors become diaphragms transmitting loads to the walls, and adequate ties are necessary between the two to accomplish this. Bond beams are used at the engineer's discretion, but vertical cracks, which may occur, will be limited to only one floor height if bond beams are employed at the floor lines.

During construction, when cross walls are used as bearing walls, each floor should be erected as if it were the first floor. The mason has to verify the wall layout continuously because the walls cannot be lined up from below since the floor hides that construction. Building walls plumb is also essential and must be continuously monitored. Occasionally, the floor system appears not to bear on the walls as intended, and it is discovered that the walls are out of line, out of plumb, or both. Since the bearing walls are designed for specific loads, including eccentricity, this can lead to wall removal in severe cases. Good practice indicates that the inspecting engineer must observe each floor placed and verify proper bearing conditions prior to floor grouting, placement of topping, or the erection of any succeeding walls above.

Wall grouting, when necessary, can be performed by the high-lift or low-lift methods. High lift is usually preferred by the contractor to expedite the work. The inspecting engineer must verify that National Concrete Masonry Association (NCMA) procedures concerning cleanouts, grout, and work quality are followed to obtain a solid wall. The grout has a high slump (9 to 12 inches) because the masonry units will absorb most of the water. When reinforcing steel is being placed, the inspector must ensure that proper lapping and embedment follow American Concrete Institute (ACI) code recommendations.

Quality control of masonry units, grout, and mortar are particularly important in engineered masonry, and there are three main laboratory compressive tests performed that relate to this type of masonry construction: the prism test, the grout cube test, and the mortar cube test. All three are prepared in the field and laboratory-tested under the guidelines of the NCMA and the American Society for Testing and Materials (ASTM). The prism test value for compressive strength coincides with the design value used in engineered masonry and is considered the most critical test by design engineers.

Masonry prisms must be stored carefully and transported only relatively short distances to the lab. The units are easily damaged, so only experienced laboratory and field technicians should handle them. Factors in selecting a lab should include the capacity of equipment to test the prisms properly, the lab's proximity to the job site, and its previous experience.

Exterior Skin

Selection of masonry materials is extremely important when using masonry as a structural element, particularly if the structure is to be a visible and integral part of the total architectural design. Where there is a possibility of expanding the facility in the future, careful consideration must be given to later availability of the original masonry units. As with foundations it is important to be able to erect structural masonry elements in nearly all bad weather conditions. Properly selecting where to use masonry as a structural component may prove the difference between a successful construction program and one plagued with delays and expensive revisions.

Building expansion joints, control joints, and isolation joints allows adjacent sections of masonry to act independently, avoiding or minimizing cracking and other failure. Expansion joints are designed to allow for thermal expansion and contraction, slight differential settlement of foundations, and, when required by the geographic location of the project, wind and earthquake forces. In order to be effective, expansion joints must be constructed and remain free from masonry debris and mortar. Exterior wall joints are commonly sealed by flexible, prefabricated joint covers. The center portion of the cover has a sponge backing for shape and to minimize condensation on the inner surface. The flanges, usually metal, are built into the masonry behind the brick wythe. Careful detailing, specification, and installation are required where such joint covers extend up the face of a parapet wall and down the inner or roof side. Expansion joints must also be properly fire-stopped so as not to compromise the building's system of fire separations.

Masonry will likely crack from shrinkage forces and minor movements of the structure. Control joints are intended to allow masonry to crack along a preplanned line, instead of cracking at random. At the brick wythe of a brick and block wall, the joint receives a resilient filler with space at the front of the joint for sealant. Concrete block control joints may be formed in two ways. For a "keyed control joint," a sash block shape is used on both sides. This provides a flat block end with a centered vertical groove. A rubber control joint key is put in the joint as the block is laid up. The key has a thickened midsection that engages the vertical grooves, and the key stops short of the face of the joint to allow space for sealant or caulking. For a "Michigan control joint," conventional blocks are used, with a recess in the block end, usually the shape of half a block core. As the wall is laid, building paper is placed against the block on one side of the joint, while the core formed by the two blocks is filled with mortar or grout. The building paper prevents the two portions of wall from bonding together, and the filled core acts as a key to keep the two portions of wall in alignment.

Isolation joints at structural members allow movement without stressing the masonry. Usually a treated corrugated boxboard is used to form a space between the member and the masonry. As with other joints, masonry debris and mortar must not be allowed to accumulate in an isolation joint or the joint becomes ineffective.

Sheet flashing materials are included under masonry work as part of a consciously planned system of internal drainage. The practical philosophy is that a wall will leak because of minute separations between mortar and masonry, porosity of mortar, and possible lapses in proper work quality. In "composite construction," a cavity occurs naturally, since the masonry units are undersized by the dimension of the mortar joints. This cavity is not parged or filled with mortar but left open to allow any infiltrated water to run down the back of the brick. In double-wythe exterior wall construction, a type of construction that naturally occurs with brick veneer but is harder to obtain in the case of exposed block because of the economic temptations to use single-wythe construction, or in composite construction, a series of through-wall flashings leads the water away from the inner wythe and out through weep holes provided immediately above the flashing at the outer wythe. These weep holes must not be sealed.

To be most effective, through-wall flashing should step down from the inner wythe to the outer wythe. This step intercepts the water, keeping it out of the inner wythe. With single-wythe walls, it is necessary to install at the flashings a course composed of two wythes of narrower units to allow this step-down.

Occasionally, the design will call for a course of brick rowlock headers as the cap for an exterior screen wall, wing wall, or parapet, instead of the more usual stone or metal coping. Experience noted by masonry associations confirms that such a detail performs poorly in climates subject to freeze-thaw cycles. Horizontal joints, being porous and subject to vagaries in work quality, allow water to penetrate the wall and freeze, loosening the rowlock bricks and even spalling the masonry below. The designer may prefer the rowlock cap because of its subtle appearance, but the specifier will argue for a stone or metal cap. If the designer prevails, the specifier may impose upon the detailer to at least slope the brick for drainage. Through-wall flashing could be shown under the rowlock course, which would protect the body of the wall from spalling, but likely at the expense of the rowlock course. Tuck-pointing the horizontal joints may increase mortar density and minimize cracks. At least, laying the rowlock course would have to be performed scrupulously.

This brief review has identified the various features of masonry systems that make their planning and scheduling so critical in a construction program. Consideration must also be given to the need for occasional deviations from what might be standard design techniques to accomplish a special construction purpose. One such frequently encountered request is to erect backup masonry early so the contractor can close in a masonry skin structure with the intent of coming back at a later date to install the veneer. Depending upon the time of year when construction is scheduled to start, it may make good sense to design an exterior wall system that permits discretionary erection of the backup independent of the exterior veneer. Naturally, appropriate anchorage, joint reinforcement, flashing, and jointing methods are preconditions to such redesign.

Another special detail may be required when masonry is to form a portion of the fire-resistant enclosure around a structural member, particularly an exterior column or spandrel. In such cases, masonry is usually to be built up around the outer or exterior flanges of a structural steel shape and spray-on fireproofing is called for on the web of the steel member. If the masonry is erected prior to fireproofing, as may be necessary in cold weather, spray-on material may be difficult to apply in the limited amount of room between the flange and the inside face of the masonry wall. In this case, alternative methods of fireproofing the member should be carefully examined to fulfill both code and construction requirements.

Insulation

The increased demands for energy conservation have led to the use of more insulation in exterior masonry walls than was formerly used. Cavity wall construction provides a space for a continuous layer of insulation, while still allowing the space to drain. The preferred material for cavity wall insulation is extruded polystyrene, now available from a number of manufacturers. Extruded polystyrene has closed cells and is not affected by water or freezing. Expanded polystyrene is available at less cost but has an open cell construction, and while being inert to moisture, the open cells allow moisture absorption and consequent loss in thermal insulating value.

Blocks are available with insulating inserts. One type of insert is a cast foam shape that does not reduce the thickness of the block web, which limits its thermal effectiveness. Another type of insert is an insulating panel fitting into recesses cast into the web. The block is available in a version with reduced web thickness, increasing the insulating efficiency at a possible loss in strength. To allow competition while precluding such a reduction in web thickness, the thermal characteristics of the former product can be specified, and the bidder may figure either product.

Poured vermiculite or perlite fill is less desirable, having even less thermal efficiency, being subject to possible water absorption in the spaces between beads, and because of the possibility of settlement. However, where cavity wall construction is precluded by the designer or because of cost and where the choice of block eliminates products with insulation inserts, poured fill may be the only solution. Two precautions are added in an attempt to minimize settlement. Pours are limited to lifts of 4 feet, allowing settlement to occur before the next lift is placed, and insect screening is placed over the cores after each lift is installed. A few inches of settlement every 4 feet may be preferable to a large void at the top of the wall. Also, if the core is punctured, the screening would allow only a 4-foot height of poured fill to be lost.

Foamed in-place insulation provides ease of application and a high thermal value. However, formulations which release objectionable fumes should be avoided. Some formulations may overcome these disadvantages. Their acceptability would depend on a record of successful applications. Infrared thermography is an effective way of verifying the uniformity and efficiency of any insulation method.

Interior Rough Work

Overall, the use of masonry must always be tempered by realizing that it is a construction system made up of many diverse, multisourced elements. The masonry unit is the basic ingredient, but used with it are all of the devices, materials, and equipment that depend upon masonry for sheathing, housing, concealment, structural support, anchorage, or enhancement. Therefore, masonry unit design always must take into account every other element that interfaces with it. Putting material or equipment in a completed masonry wall is tedious, time-consuming, and often destructive. The best time to think about what must be built into a brick or block wall is when it is being designed, rather than when it is being bid, or even worse, being erected.

Take the instance when a contract for all project masonry is let early, along with the contracts for concrete and structural steel. The desired result of expediting early procurement and installation of masonry appears satisfied, at least on the surface. However, the instant that masonry erection starts, it will become apparent that one needs a plumber, an electrician, a carpenter, a miscellaneous iron erector, and perhaps even other trades people along with the materials they are to install on the job to permit effective continuity of masonry construction. Toothing-out a wall for later installation of hollow metal or elevator door frames, or omitting a wall until a subsequent plumbing contract can be let and the contractor and material is on the job, becomes expensive and disruptive. The architect and contractor must carefully think through the construction sequence to avoid attempting to commence masonry construction with inadequate representation of other involved trades.

Another serious problem encountered in wall design is the improper sizing of openings to permit setting or servicing of equipment. Although this sounds like a strange occurrence, it unfortunately is a common mistake, sometimes made several times within any one project. It is the duty of the design team to ensure that a fully coordinated and knit-together design is produced. The special problem that inaccurate opening definition brings when the wall is masonry is that it is more difficult, and often more expensive, to revise masonry once erected than to rework some of the lighter forms of wall construction such as dry wall or even plaster. Therefore, when using masonry, opening dimensions in walls must be carefully defined and checked thoroughly and repeatedly throughout the design period.

Such dimensional errors most frequently occur at equipment rooms, functional and service spaces, and in special purpose areas in institutional installations where accurate sizes of food service or sterilizing equipment are sometimes difficult to obtain prior to an award of a contract. It is the obligation of the masonry design team to provide adequate access to all areas where entry must be had through a wall.

Finishes

During construction it is crucial to avoid undue or overlong exposure of finished surfaces to construction traffic and weather. So, the use of structural exposed finish masonry which must be erected early in the job sequence must be done selectively and carefully. If the surface of the masonry is susceptible to damage during subsequent construction, there is a good chance that it will be damaged, particularly if exposed surfaces, edges, and corners are not adequately protected. Replacement of damaged masonry surfaces is, at best, difficult, and even careful repairs usually become conspicuous after weathering.

The need to avoid premature finish material installation is not limited to vertical masonry systems. Those areas that receive ceramic or quarry tile or window details that call for slate or similar stools should be designed in such fashion that early installation is not required if there is a possibility of in-place damage. Although it is the fundamental responsibility of the contractor to protect work, in any properly operated construction program work protection must be shared by those responsible for selecting the material and specifying the method and sequence of its installation.

When masonry is used as a horizontal covering material, such as for floors, the conditions under which it is to be installed should be considered along with selection criteria based on appearance and wearing characteristics. When most floor masonry materials are laid, they are usually exposed to construction traffic damage and as such can interfere with field operation sequences. Normally there is little that can be done about such sequencing during the design process, but both architect and contractor should be sensitive to this problem once contracts are let. Prompt submissions and timely approvals, which encourage careful scheduling of deliveries of such material, will give field forces a time range into which the material installation can best be fitted. Frequently, installation of these materials must be sandwiched into a very narrow time window, and missing that schedule through late delivery of material can intensify the potential disruption or damage that might be caused by its later installation.

It is important to be aware that field assembly of masonry elements is still done manually. When the opportunity arises for timely and effective placement in the field operation, having the material on hand at the right time may spell the difference between success and failure in the use of a masonry system.

Prefabricated Masonry Systems

In the 1960s and early 1970s, there was considerable interest in prefabricated masonry for lintels, soffits, and wall panels. In addition, high-bond mortar allowed walls only a single brick in thickness, perforated screen walls, hanging brick, and a new series of shapes, forms, and configurations that only the designer's mind could create.

On one project, the basis of the bid was to be a prefabricated exterior wall system, with floor-to-floor panels a single brick wythe in thickness, prefabricated from brick and high-bond mortar and erected in the manner of precast concrete panels. Interior finishes would be applied to furring over the interior face of the panels. Panel details and sizes were worked out with a local fabricator, who had to consider the clearances under bridges on the way from the fabricating yard to the site, among other limitations. To verify that the prefabricated system would be economical, an alternate system was proposed which would allow field-laid masonry in lieu of prefabricated panels. The alternate included an inner wythe of concrete block, necessary only in the case of field-laid masonry. During the bidding process it became apparent to the fabricator, as well as to other bidders, that because of the large variety in panel sizes and other aspects of prefabrication, it would be less expensive to field-erect the exterior walls, even including the cost of the added inner wythe. The project was built according to the alternate bid in conventional masonry construction, but had it been possible to achieve more uniformity in panels, the prefabricated solution would have been competitive.

On that project, the alternate retained certain prefabricated lintels, but without the use of high-bond mortar. These prefabricated lintels consisted of a row of brick headers with two threaded stainless steel rods protruding through the top of the lintel. Holes were cut in the supporting steel above, and the lintels were shimmed and fastened in place with nuts. During erection, some of the threaded rods broke below the nuts. Investigations showed that the rods were more than adequately designed, but that unusual erection stresses were incurred. The contractor was drawing the lintels into final alignment by turning the nuts. In some cases only one rod was secured, with that end of the lintel pushing up tight to the steel above. The lintel acted as a fulcrum, with its own weight multiplied sufficiently to overstress the rod. With more care in erection, the project was completed without further difficulties.

Another project included similar prefabricated brick lintels, but used both high-bond mortar with a latex polymer-type additive and steel reinforcing through the cores of the header bricks. A few years after completion of the building, rust-stained cracks appeared in a number of the lintels, running through several bricks and intervening mortar, parallel to the direction of the reinforcing. A lintel was removed and saw-cut. There was extreme rusting of the reinforcing rods, expanding their size and consequently stressing the brick and mortar to failure. As a crack opened, corrosion accelerated. Such rusting was unusual and unanticipated in masonry construction, where accepted practice relied on the natural alkalinity of the mortar which usually inhibits rusting. After testing it was felt that some component of the high-bond mortar additive may have become liberated, destroying the alkalinity of the mortar and fostering galvanic corrosion. As a solution, a portion of the removed lintel was pressure-injected with epoxy along the cracks, and further saw cutting revealed that the epoxy had migrated thoroughly through the cracks, encapsulating the steel. The remaining cracked lintels were injected with epoxy and the solution appears to be permanent. Lintels are to be inspected every few years with any new cracks to be epoxy-injected.

Prefabrication of masonry still appears to be a viable solution, but clearly it poses a new dimension in designing to achieve maximum uniformity, with consequent cost savings due to duplication, and in the careful selection of materials, in order to avoid new and unusual problems of construction or maintenance.

Preparation of Construction Documents

In today's construction business it is frequently found that the phased release of the contract documents is desirable to maintain needed project progress. In such cases selection of the contract package in which masonry is to be provided and erected must properly be made early by the design team. When involved in the project during design, the contractor should also take part in making that decision.

Not only must items that are built into masonry be carefully planned, but also those that directly adjoin masonry elements which could cause erection interruptions and delays. For example, at the roof of a building where masonry is used as an exterior material, the nailer, blocking, insulation, and roofing sheet metal system might be designed to allow the mason to complete work even though a roofer or a metal deck erector was not on the job by the time of completion of exterior masonry units.

When one considers that a masonry wall might contain hollow metal frames, structural steel columns, electrical conduit, mechanical piping, panel boxes, sheet metal ductwork, miscellaneous iron and pipe sleeves, plus an almost unlimited variety of other kinds of construction materials and equipment, the need for careful early planning becomes apparent.

A review of sections and details should always be made wherever masonry interfaces or touches another material whose installation depends upon the masonry sequencing. The versatility of masonry materials generally allows for accommodating erection interfaces of this type. Only when a design and sequencing dysfunction is allowed to occur in the awarding of contracts or the procurement of materials may such interfaces prove difficult.

Award of Contracts

Award of contracts and procurement of masonry materials should be given close attention when masonry is used in the exposed areas of the building. A most important item is to ensure that consistency of appearance throughout the facility is maintained by proper ordering of the units. Masonry color and texture vary from manufacturer to manufacturer, kiln to kiln, and firing to firing. Recently, for instance, a large project which had sizable amounts of exposed exterior masonry was to be brought on line in successive stages through the award of three separate architectural contracts. These contracts were also to be awarded at different times during the project. This meant that masonry for all three major contract units probably would have to be purchased early and from one supplier, so as to maintain uniformity of appearance.

Although this problem appears obvious, its resolution and the implementation of the solution were difficult. Masonry procurement contracts had to be awarded along with award of the first of the three major contracts. Thus, special consideration had to be given to soliciting separate proposals for masonry units and to devise a suitable technique by which the delivered masonry could be stored and then ultimately allocated to each unit contractor. This matter was one that had to be resolved prior to the issue of the first of the contracts and demanded architectural design decisions on all areas very early in the project.

Procurement

The need for careful attention to procurement of masonry is evident from the examples already discussed. However, a brief review of the sequences usually followed in procurement would be of help in understanding better how important proper scheduling and planning are for efficient masonry use.

Procurement usually begins for the designer with a submittal. This may be a cut, a shop drawing, a sample, a color chip, range samples of masonry materials, or almost any kind of document or sample that allows the architect and owner to authorize proceeding further with the procurement process. Since the next step after submittals and ultimate approval usually involves committing sizable amounts of money, requirements for the content and form of submittals for masonry materials must be described clearly in the construction contract documents. The designer should also make absolutely certain that the materials specified are available. It is unfortunate, but true, that often the contractor encounters the situation where a specified masonry material, particularly in hard tiles, is no longer manufactured. This oversight usually creates delays at a most critical time and a time-consuming reselection may have to be made.

Once masonry materials are selected, sample walls or mock-ups of the units to be used are built by the contractor to confirm the color, texture, and quality of the masonry units and the work quality and color of the mortar. Ideally, the mortar coloring pigment should be from the batch that is purchased and manufactured for this project alone and not from a warehouse or from a standard lot. Proper location of the mock-up is also important. The architect should select locations that provide the expected final light conditions needed to adequately evaluate the sample wall. There have been occasions where poorly selected locations have had to be changed several times, resulting in expensive moves of the wall panel and even reconstruction of the panel to permit an additional evaluation to be made.

After submittals and mock-ups are completed and reviewed, it is the obligation of the design team and the owner to approve promptly or to revise and fully explain what is wanted. Delays to approvals, particularly where masonry is part of the structural frame, can cause serious domino effects on construction progress. Once the full process of procurements is initiated, delays must be kept to an absolute minimum if good relations are to be maintained and economical practices are to be followed in the field.

Once approvals are obtained, the manufacture of the units is released, and from that point, revisions of any type become very expensive. Of importance after release, and with responsibility resting primarily with the contractor, is the need to assure adequate storage space on the site once masonry materials begin arriving. Although most materials used in construction are bulky and difficult to store, the nature and weight of masonry generally make certain amounts of extra handling necessary. In conjunction with the owner and the architect, the contractor has an obligation to help locate and set aside a suitable storage space for the masonry if it is not to be used as it arrives at the job site, to minimize this extra effort.

Although newly received brick at the job site is difficult (if not impossible) to inspect for appropriate range and color, the designer should understand that differing methods of packaging brick may require the mason to have direction from the designer as to how to draw the masonry units from the stockpile. Several years ago a shopping center was being entirely faced with a moderate range brick. Erection of the brick began with only minimal attention from the architect and owner. It was apparent after four or five days of work that the brick had been palletized, with each pallet being loaded with masonry of the same color. Thus, the walls as erected consisted first of all masonry units of one tone with succeeding lifts each having masonry units with the next range of color. Fortunately the error was discovered early and a proper pallet blend initiated that ensured that the material color range was properly allocated over the building face.

Careful selection of masonry materials is also important to assure chemical compatibility of components in the structure. Already mentioned was a recent instance when reactions between various types of mortar, esoteric mortar additives, masonry materials, and built-in metallic elements were destructive to the system because of deterioration of hidden anchoring or reinforcing surfaces. In another instance, masonry units commonly used in one geographic area were introduced into another area having different weather conditions, resulting in staining and deterioration due to accelerated weathering. Material specifications must be closely coordinated with both architectural and structural intent to ensure that compatibility is maintained.

During procurement it is also important to understand the potential difficulty in acquiring special masonry shapes. Here it is an obligation of the architect and the contractor to ensure that well-defined submittal processes are followed carefully and prompt approvals are given. Special masonry shapes, although more costly, have the inherent potential to create interesting forms and configurations. Unique sizes, angles, or configurations will sometimes make it necessary to obtain early approval and acceptance of a submittal so the special unit can be fired along with the typical units.

Installation

Once the procurement process has been completed and masonry materials are on the job and available, installation should proceed with minimal delays, unless problems arise that are unforeseen during the design process. It should be remembered that as a structural unit, masonry may have very little capacity to carry unusual construction loads prior to having all structural components in place. Therefore, its interim structural capabilities are often a source of field concern to the contractor who may need help from the architect and engineer in determining what construction support and bracing measures should be taken.

Bracing for masonry walls is usually space-consuming, and if delays to installation of permanent structural members are encountered, such bracing may interfere with succeeding activities. On one school project, the necessary bracing for a high brick bearing wall had to be left in place for such a long period that it prevented timely correction required of a floor slab prior to installation of topping. The delay to corrective action took the project into winter and prevented such work from being done during good weather. Although in this case the delay was the fault of the contractor, not the design team, the incident illustrates the need for properly planning and scheduling masonry erection.

Whenever possible, it is advisable to obtain preconstruction testing of the materials to be used to provide guidelines for the work to follow. As with any testing, by the time field test results are known, construction has usually progressed to a point that makes repair or removal extremely costly and in some cases almost prohibitive. If doubt exists, it is advisable to take more test samples and obtain early test results. For instance, masonry tests for the lower floors of a multistory building can be obtained at anywhere from two to five days, in addition to the normal seven and twenty-eight days. There may also be times when such results are desired at fourteen days and such extra samples will allow for this.

Several aspects of masonry should be mentioned. For resistance to moisture penetration, brick should be laid in a full bed of mortar, rather than a furrowed bed. The end of the brick should be covered with enough mortar so that when the brick is placed the mortar squeezes out of the joint. This assures the full head joint essential to resist water penetration.

Concrete block usually needs full face shell mortaring only, but in certain locations in a wall, such as the starter courses, top courses, and bearing courses, the webs should be bedded in mortar also. Cores to be grouted, cavities, and expansion joints should be kept free from mortar droppings.

For best weather resistance, joints should be tooled concave or to a

V profile. This increases the surface density of the mortar, making it less porous, and imparts a profile which sheds water. Raked joints have relatively poor weather resistance.

Mortar mixing and proportioning are usually specified as conforming to American Society for Testing and Materials (ASTM) C270, with a prohibition against or limitation of chlorides and accelerators. Mortar types are specified by minimum strengths and by proportion, allowing either masonry cement or lime in various combinations with portland cement. (The appendix to ASTM C270 includes a discussion of the mortar types required for various uses.) The engineer may require a stronger mortar for structural purposes, but care should be exercised since it is evident that the stronger the mortar, the less workable it is and the less watertight the wall may be. Weaker mortars contain greater amounts of lime or masonry cement, both of which exhibit an "autogenous healing" process which seals small cracks. Various regions of the country may favor mortar mixes which include lime, while other regions may favor mixes including masonry cement, depending on availability.

Grouts for reinforced masonry and for grouted cores are specified per ASTM C476 and may be furnished in the manner of ready-mixed concrete. Proportions include aggregates appropriate to the size of the spaces grouted.

Pigmented mortar may be required for brick or integrally colored block to meet the design intent. Good practice usually restricts pigments to the use of prepackaged colored mortar or the addition of prepackaged pigment, one package per batch, to prepackaged mortar, with all pigment for a project manufactured in one lot. Proportions should remain constant for color control, and mixing procedures should be reviewed with the architect and the representative of the manufacturer. Mortar for glazed block may require stearates to impart moisture repellency.

For good masonry installation practice, it should be remembered that it may be difficult for the mason in the field to know exactly what the architect had in mind during the design process. Thus, the responsibility for monitoring early masonry construction to ensure adherence to desired appearance and practice standards is one that rests primarily upon the architect.

Maintenance

We have focused in this brief discussion on the relation of masonry design and installation to the construction planning and scheduling process. Once the project is built, turned over, and the maintenance period begins, the responsibility of the designer in the proper selection of the components enters a most critical phase.

Every good masonry design must take into account the nature of what happens to the hidden elements within the wall systems as the facility ages. Masonry buildings will usually exhibit wall cracks, and this is particularly true of mid- to high-rise structures that are wall bearing. These cracks can occur for various reasons, some of the more common being differential settlement of foundations, work quality, location and construction of expansion, control and isolation joints, lack of reinforcing, incompatibility of materials, the building shape, environmental conditions during construction, and structural details.

Care should be taken with structural details of wall-to-wall connections; *only* flexible anchors should be utilized and masonry control joints should be carefully discussed with the contractor in the field.

Of particular concern are critical structural supports, anchors, and inserts. The impact of a major masonry repair owing to deterioration of structural anchorages can often be avoided by the architect being fully aware of the deteriorating factors present in the masonry environment. Most designers today know of the availability of various metals commonly used now in masonry anchorages. Hence, this problem is not as widespread today as it was in the past. Nevertheless, design and construction responsibility remains to ascertain that masonry components will function compatibly during use as they were intended to function.

In summary, the good masonry designer should remember

1. That masonry is a material almost always used in conjunction with a multitude of other materials. Knowledge of good masonry construction demands knowledge of how each of these other materials is built in or attached to the masonry and how they behave together.

2. That a masonry wall is not built only by masons but also by plumbers, electricians, iron workers, carpenters, and roofers, to name only a few. Each installation must be considered during design.

3. That masonry, like all building materials, has its scheduling limitations. Designing within those limitations permits concentration on excellence of use while still allowing great diversity of design.

4. That today's construction business is more closely connected to design than ever before. This working together of the designer, constructor, owner, and user should make possible a molding of talents that, properly managed, will result in superior buildings.

5. That elements of plan, schedule, cost, and quality dominate after the design is finalized. In specifying masonry it is imperative that the designer participate fully in the process of submittal, approval, manufacture, delivery, and ultimate installation of the material.

One secret of good design is identified as the ability of the designer to understand the total process of design and construction without separating one from the other by artificial responsibility lines. With masonry materials we find that the expert designer is invariably one who fully understands and is sympathetic to the construction advantages, features, and limitations of the materials from which the designs are produced. This is perhaps more true of masonry than any other construction material in common use today.

Following these guidelines should make it possible for the architect, engineer, and contractor to improve their field planning and scheduling of masonry systems installation and, in turn, to enhance greatly their ability to work with this wonderfully versatile material.

Appendix

T he following is a list of contributing organizations who may be contacted
for technical and practical information on masonry construction.

MASONRY STATE INSTITUTES

Colorado Masonry Institute
3003 East Third Avenue, S-301
Denver, CO 80206
(303) 321-2141

Masonry Institute of Atlanta
59 Chaumont Sq. N.W.
Atlanta, GA 30327
(404) 352-2727

Illinois Masonry Institute
1550 Northwest Highway, S.201
Park Ridge, IL 60068
(312) 694-2737

Ohio Masonry Council
1737 Euclid Avenue
Suite 210
Cleveland, OH 44115
(216) 781-7740

Masonry Institute of Michigan, Inc.
24155 Drake Road, S-202
Farmington, MI 48024
(313) 478-6455

Masonry Institute of St. Louis
1429 S. Big Bend Boulevard
St. Louis, MO 63117
(314) 645-5888

Delaware Valley Masonry Institute
134 North Narberth Avenue
Narberth, PA 19072
(315) 839-3864

Masonry Institute of Tennessee
5575 Poplar, S-422
Memphis, TN 38119
(901) 725-7990

NATIONAL MASONRY INSTITUTES

Brick Institute of America
1750 Old Meadow Road
McLean, Virginia 22102
Publishers of "Technical Notes on Brick
 Construction"

National Concrete Masonry Association
2302 Horse Pen Road
P.O. Box 781
Herndon, VA 22070
PUBLICATIONS: Guide Specification for
 Concrete Masonry

International Masonry Institute
823 15th Street N.W.
Washington D.C. 20005

INTERNATIONAL MASONRY ASSOCIATIONS

Belgium
Nationale Greopering der Klei Nijverheid
Viskopers Straat 13, Bus 22, 1000 Brussel, Belgium

Atelier D'Architecture, Mr. Lucien Kroll (Brick Art)
Av. L. Berlaimont 20/BT9
B 1160 Bruxelles, Belgium

Denis Van Impe, Architect (Brick Art)
Predikhereniel 3
B 9000 Ghent, Belgium

England	Brick Development Association Woodside House, Winkfield, Windsor Berkshire SL4 2DX, England
France	Federation des Fabricants de Tuiles et de Briques de France 17 rue Letellier 75015, Paris, France
Holland	De Nederlandse Baksteen Industrie, Hoofdstraat 8, 6994 AE De Steeg, Holland
Italy	Associazione Nazionale Degli Industriali Dei Laterizi Via Cavour 71 00184 Rome, Italy
Norway	Mur Senfret nedre Vollgt 1, Oslo 1, Norway
South Africa	Brick Development Association of S.A. LTD. 502 Datakor House/Gebou 502 Cr/Hu Smit & DeBeer Str. Braamfontein Johannesburg 2001 31156 Braamfontein 2017, South Africa
United States	International Brick Collectors' Association 10942 Montego Drive San Diego, CA 92124

Photographers

Index

ABOUT THE AUTHOR

Louis G. Redstone, FAIA, an internationally recognized architectural authority, began his love affair with masonry at an early age, right after high school. As he relates, "I joined a group of young people going to Palestine, and I was part of a construction training group working under the tutelage of an Egyptian master mason. For three years, I learned the intricacies of working with stone and brick."

This early training has served him well over the years. A member of the leading professional and academic societies, Mr. Redstone is the recipient of awards and medals from the AIA, the National Society of Interior Designers, and other organizations. He is the author of such respected books as *Art in Architecture, New Dimensions in Shopping Centers and Stores, The New Downtowns,* and *Public Art: New Directions.* He is also the editor of *Hospitals and Health Care Facilities* and *Institutional Buildings.* All are published by McGraw-Hill.

After returning from Palestine, Louis G. Redstone received his B.S. degree in architecture from the University of Michigan and his Masters degree in architecture and urban design from the Cranbrook Academy of Art. Today, Mr. Redstone heads his own award-winning architectural firm. And throughout his close to fifty years of active practice, masonry has been part of his professional "trademark."